About the Author

SHAHRAM AKBARZADEH is a Senior Lecturer in Global Politics at the School of Political and Social Inquiry, Monash University, Australia. He has researched and published on Central Asian affairs for a decade. Dr Akbarzadeh has co-authored the *Historical Dictionary of Tajikistan* (Scarecrow Press, 2002) and co-edited *Muslim Communities in Australia* (University of New South Wales Press, 2001), *Islam and Political Legitimacy* (Routledge/Curzon, 2003), and *Islam and the West: Reflections from Australia* (UNSW Press, 2005).

Uzbekistan and the United States

Authoritarianism, Islamism and Washington's Security Agenda

SHAHRAM AKBARZADEH

ZED BOOKS
London & New York

For Mozhgan, Pasha and Nikoo

Uzbekistan and the United States was first published in 2005 by
Zed Books Ltd, 7 Cynthia Street, London N1 9JF, UK,
and Room 400, 175 Fifth Avenue, New York, NY 10010, USA

www.zedbooks.co.uk

Designed and typeset in Monotype Joanna by Illuminati, Grosmont
Cover designed by Andrew Corbett
Printed and bound in Malta by Gutenberg Press Ltd

Distributed in the USA exclusively by Palgrave Macmillan,
a division of St Martin's Press, LLC, 175 Fifth Avenue, New York, NY 10010

A catalogue record for this book is available from the British Library
Library of Congress Cataloging-in-Publication Data available

ISBN 1 84277 422 0 (Hb)
ISBN 1 84277 423 9 (Pb)

Contents

Acknowledgements

This project was made possible by the generous support of the Australian Research Council, the Faculty of Arts Research Initiative Grant Scheme at Monash University, and the Global Terrorism Research Unit at the School of Political and Social Inquiry at Monash University. I am indebted to Ms Elena Mogilevski for her systematic and meticulous collection and presentation of the primary sources, and her skills in locating rare documents. I also wish to register my gratitude to Professor John Miller (La Trobe University) for introducing me to Central Asia and putting up with my wide-eyed approach to the region during my doctoral studies; Professor Joseph Camilleri (La Trobe University) for rekindling my interest in Central Asia and providing much needed intellectual stimulation to sustain me over the course of research and writing for the present study; Assistant Professor Pauline Jones Luong (University of Yale) for her generosity of spirit and practical suggestions to improve this book; and Professor Yaacov Ro'i (University of Tel Aviv) for spending much more time on studying the entire book than I ever expected, offering many helpful tips, and accepting the invitation to write the Foreword. I am grateful for all this support and encouragement. As per the usual caveat, I bear sole responsibility for the content of this book.

Chronology

1918		Formation of the Turkestan Soviet Republic, covering most of Central Asia, with its capital in Tashkent.
1924		Formation of the Uzbek Soviet Socialist Republic, including the Tajik Autonomous Soviet Socialist Republic (TASSR).
1929		The emergences of the present borders of Uzbekistan following the removal of the TASSR from Tashkent's jurisdiction.
1989		Islam Karimov becomes first secretary of the Communist Party of Uzbekistan.
1990	March	Islam Karimov elected president by the Supreme Soviet of Uzbekistan.
1991	August	Declaration of independence by the Supreme Soviet of Uzbekistan (31 August).
1991	November	Communist Party of Uzbekistan is renamed the People's Democratic Party of Uzbekistan (PDPU).
1991	December	Uzbekistan joins the Commonwealth of Independent States (CIS).
1991	December	The incumbent Islam Karimov wins the first direct presidential election in the history of Uzbekistan against Muhammad Solih, leader of the opposition Erk Democratic Party.
1992	May	Onset of civil war in neighbouring Tajikistan.

1992	May	Formation of the CIS Collective Security Treaty with Uzbekistan as a founding member.
1992	December	Uzbekistan adopts its post-Soviet constitution, which grants the president extensive powers and adopts indigenous names for state institutions: the parliament is called the Oliy Majlis (Supreme Assembly).
1994	July	Uzbekistan joins the Nato Partnership for Peace (PfP) programme.
1994	December	The first post-Soviet parliamentary elections for the Oliy Majlis.
1995	December	Uzbekistan joins Kyrgyzstan and Kazakhstan in forming the Central Asian Battalion (Centrazbat) as a peacekeeping force within the framework of Nato PfP.
1996	March	President Islam Karimov's term extended for another five years.
1996	September	Fall of Kabul to Taliban forces.
1999	February	Bombing in Tashkent, blamed on the Islamic Movement of Uzbekistan and Muhammad Solih, the exiled leader of Erk.
1999	April	Uzbekistan refuses to renew its membership of the CIS Collective Security Treaty (2 April)
1999	April	Uzbekistan joins Georgia, Ukraine, Azerbaijan and Moldova in GUUAM (24 April).
1999	August	The first armed incursion by the Islamic Movement of Uzbekistan (IMU) into the Batken region of Kyrgyzstan.
1999	December	Parliamentary elections for the Oliy Majlis.
2000	January	Islam Karimov wins a landslide victory in direct presidential elections, criticised by Western observers as 'not free'.
2000	July	Uzbekistan attends the Dushanbe Summit of the Shanghai Forum as observer.
2000	August	IMU conducts multiple incursions into southern Kyrgyzstan.
2001	June	Uzbekistan becomes a full member the Shanghai group, leading to its renaming as the Shanghai Cooperation Organisation (SCO).

2001	July	IMU forces attack television station in the Batken region of Kyrgyzstan.
2001	September	First US troops arrive in Uzbekistan as part of the 'war on terror'.
2002	January	Referendum extends Karimov's presidential term to 2007.
2002	March	Signing of the US–Uzbek Declaration on Strategic Partnership.
2002	May	Media censorship officially abolished.
2002	June	Uzbekistan declares intention to leave GUUAM but is dissuaded by the United States.
2003	March	Tashkent declares support for the US-led attack on Iraq.
2005	September	The SCO makes a surprise announcement about plans to establish an anti-terrorist centre in Tashkent.

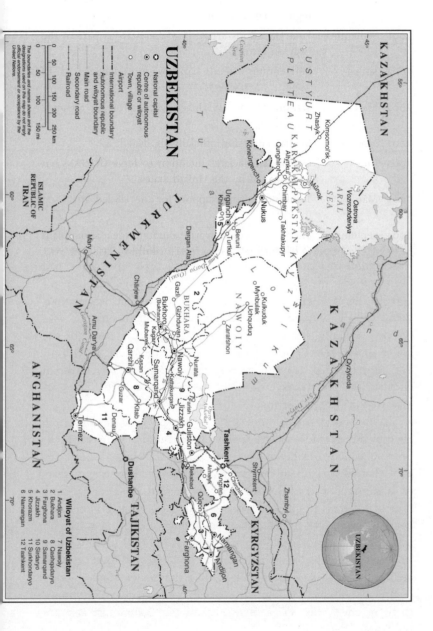

Foreword

Uzbekistan emerged from relative obscurity following the American intervention in Central Asia in the wake of September 11. It had been independent for exactly a decade by this time, but had not been in the limelight, its birth pangs and subsequent deliberations going mostly unnoticed by a world whose main attention was directed towards developments in Russia itself and some of the better-known post-Communist states in central and eastern Europe. The American-led coalition's campaign in Afghanistan, however, changed the picture as Uzbekistan hastened to take the place of Washington's central partner in the region.

Shahram Akbarzadeh's book seeks to explain how this occurred. He provides a comprehensive review of the country's domestic background, which provides one of the keys to Uzbekistan's problems as it charted its path in the international arena after seventy years of existence as part of the Soviet Union. Indeed, the country came into being with its present name and in its current borders as a consequence of the Bolsheviks' nationalities policy and had no tradition of autonomous foreign policymaking. But, perhaps more importantly, it had no experience in conducting its own internal affairs and economy, for although, like the Soviet Union's other component union republics, it officially had its own Communist Party, in effect this was a mere filial of the Communist Party of the Soviet Union.

Uzbekistan is a country with considerably more than 20 million inhabitants, nearly 75 per cent of whom are ethnic Uzbeks. Most of the other nationalities represented in its population are also indigenous to Central Asia and are traditionally Muslim in faith and culture. Moreover, there are significant Uzbek populations in the four other Central Asian successor states, as well as in Afghanistan, so that Uzbekistan is not just the most populous of Central Asia's states and geographically the linchpin of the region, but comprises a major factor in all its political dilemmas, as has been evident from the evolution of independent Tajikistan and Kyrgyzstan.

Nor is Uzbekistan itself a homogeneous society. The provinces that comprise the Uzbek part of the Ferghana Valley – a region divided between Uzbekistan, Tajikistan and Kyrgyzstan – are in many ways an entity unto themselves. With one of the world's densest populations, the Ferghana Valley has traditionally been the most ardently Islamic of the country's regions and the centre of opposition to Tashkent's ruling cliques. Since independence, the Ferghana Valley, with its lower standard of living, has been the focus of social and political dissatisfaction, even though in Karimov's Uzbekistan there have been very few opportunities to give vent to major discontent.

The main channel for political opposition has been Islam since President Islam Karimov foreclosed all possibilities for political opposition per se. Akbarzadeh has gone to great pains to explain the various Islamic forces, particularly the two radical organisations which the Karimov regime has sought to eradicate: the Islamic Movement of Uzbekistan (the IMU) and Hizb al-Tahrir al-Islami (the Party of Islamic Liberation), known simply as Hizb ut-Tahrir in Uzbekistan. From this book, it becomes clear how Karimov's policy misfired and, instead of taming Islam, the Uzbekistan government catapulted Islamists into ever more extreme positions. Through persistent persecution, it convinced them, first, that they had no chance of making headway except by radicalising, and, second, that they had nothing to lose by adopting a militant stance since they were, a priori, targeted for repression.

The insistence of the Karimov regime upon authoritarianism and the consequent denial of human rights and freedoms threatened to obstruct Uzbekistan's foreign relations and particularly its likelihood of obtaining economic aid. Indeed, prior to September 11, the financial assistance it received from the West was limited, largely as a result of pressure on Western organisations and governments on the part of human right groups and lobbies. This changed after the attack on the Twin Towers and the Pentagon, which seemed, as it were, to give legitimacy to Uzbekistan's claims regarding the danger to domestic and regional security from Islamic activism. Karimov's statements of support for the United States and his keenness to enter the US-led coalition answered an urgent American need for facilities on Afghanistan's northern border. The common strategic interest of the war against terror shifted the Uzbekistan regime's violations of human rights to the background and made them seemingly ancillary. Karimov's policies received their ultimate legitimisation.

This is the story told by Shahram Akbarzadeh, one that is surely important for those interested in Central Asia, whether as scholars or as businessmen and decision-makers. His exposé is also pertinent for anyone who would like to believe that the United States has learned a lesson from its earlier de facto vindication of regimes, particularly in Asia, which flouted all those norms that American political culture seemed to make precious. It is agreed that the war against terror is a paramount need in the early twenty-first century. Yet surely it must not and cannot be promoted and conducted at the expense of the individual and collective rights of entire populations. Even if all wars dictate diversions from the optimal pursuit of government policy, there have to be red lines which must not be crossed and which democratic states and governments cannot condone.

Yaacov Ro'i,
Professor of Central Asian Studies,
University of Tel Aviv

Introduction

In the aftermath of the September 11 attacks, Uzbekistan suddenly found itself courted by the United States. The common fear of Islamic extremism pushed aside earlier stumbling blocks to closer bilateral relations. US concerns with the slow pace of democratic reforms in Uzbekistan were relegated to the periphery. The signing of the US–Uzbek Declaration of Strategic Partnership in March 2002 confirmed the shift in US policy towards Uzbekistan. Fighting Islamic extremism became the catalyst for the US–Uzbek rapprochement. In the process Uzbekistan's poor human rights record and the absence of political reforms have become significantly less pivotal in defining Washington's approach to this Central Asian state. This policy shift has helped relieve international pressure on Uzbek authorities to implement reforms. It is, of course, difficult to argue that the US prioritisation of democratic reforms in the first decade of Uzbekistan's independence made a significant impact on the Uzbek domestic scene. But it may be stated with certainty that the current downplaying of US concerns with democratisation would only embolden the Uzbek leadership under President Islam Karimov, which has shown no inclination towards making itself accountable to the citizens of Uzbekistan.

Uzbekistan's political system is best defined as authoritarian. The Uzbek leadership, under President Islam Karimov, has maintained a tight grip on political activity in Uzbekistan. This has been achieved through a combination of judicial and extrajudicial harassment and elimination of its opponents, and the use of general notions of nationalism and the promotion of indigenous traditions to gain public legitimacy. The Soviet collapse did not lead to democratisation in Uzbekistan. Instead the leadership went through an important phase in 1991–92 which at best may be described as a 'training period'. It cautiously, and somewhat reluctantly, experimented with a nascent political pluralism while erecting new barriers to confine socio-political forces and defend itself against any serious challenge to its authority. By 1993 the regime had managed to construct a multiparty façade for its essentially intolerant behaviour towards political dissent. The evolution of authoritarianism in Uzbekistan, and its acceptance in the international community, were inseparable from the debate about Islamic radicalism. President Karimov's leadership made systematic use of the alleged threat posed by political Islam to justify measures that curtailed political freedom. Political Islam, or Islamism, as a political ideology committed to the capture and Islamisation of the state, the authorities told their citizens and the international community, was a real danger. The experience of the Islamic Revolution in Iran, the civil war in Tajikistan and the emergence of the Taliban movement in Afghanistan were recounted by the authorities in Tashkent to point to the ominous 'Islamic threat' to stability in Uzbekistan and Central Asia as a whole.

The 'war on terror' was a blessing for Uzbek leaders. They had repeatedly called for international action against Islamic extremism and fanaticism. Tashkent was especially anxious about the developments in Afghanistan after the ascendancy of the Taliban to power. The fall of Kabul led to a Central Asia–Russia summit in October 1996 where President Karimov called for a unified policy in preparation for an anticipated Taliban advance northward.[1] In an interview with the Russian daily *Komsomol'skaya Pravda*, he elaborated on his idea of united action by emphasising the capabilities of General Abdul Rashid Dostum to stop the Taliban from reaching the borders of Central Asia.[2] President Karimov later raised his concerns with the visiting president of Pakistan, Farooq Ahmad Khan Leghari.[3] President Karimov was concerned that the Taliban threat would be used as a pretext for Russia's military presence in Central Asia, and rejected offers of help from Moscow to bolster its border control. According to Uzbek officials interviewed by the Russian press, the Taliban would not be able to break the 'Karimov line' of defence.[4]

Despite Uzbekistan's show of self-sufficiency in protecting its borders, President Karimov did not hide the fact that Uzbekistan could not address the so-called Islamic threat alone. The growth of Islamist groups in the latter part of the 1990s, with ties that extended beyond the national boundaries of Uzbekistan, was a poignant example of the extra-national magnitude of the challenge facing the authorities. It seemed as though the imaginary Islamic threat was becoming a reality in the second half of the 1990s.[5] As will be discussed in Chapter 2, the emergence of the Islamic Movement of Uzbekistan and Hizb ut-Tahrir served as a reminder to Uzbek leaders that even the slightest easing of state control over public life could lead to the proliferation of radical Islamic groups and unpredictable consequences.

The obsession with the Islamic threat, routinely exaggerated by Uzbek officials and the media, became paramount in Uzbekistan's foreign policy. Chapter 3 traces Tashkent's overtures to a number of regional organisations which the authorities hoped would strengthen Uzbekistan's position internally and internationally, first, against Islamic insurgents and, second, against Moscow. These two objectives, however, did not always coincide and seldom allowed Uzbekistan to pursue a consistent foreign policy. Tashkent's admission to the anti-Russian group of GUUAM (a regional organisation named after its members: Georgia, Ukraine, Uzbekistan, Azerbaijan and Moldova), and the subsequent entry into the Shanghai Cooperation Organisation (SCO), signified the Uzbek leadership's attempt to pursue two competing objectives. GUUAM was aimed at countering the Russian influence, while the SCO had Islamic insurgency in its sights. But it was really the post-September 11 partnership with the United States that offered the best chance to Tashkent of pursuing both goals in tandem.

Chapter 4 examines the history of relations between Uzbekistan and the United States. US policy on Uzbekistan was marked by a cautious approach that kept Uzbekistan at arms length. The failure of the Uzbek leadership to heed international calls for democratisation was a major issue influencing US policy. The other determining factor was Russia and its attitude to close US ties with Central Asia as an encroachment on its backyard. Both Republican and Democrat administrations were concerned about the negative repercussions of establishing close relations with the authoritarian regimes on Russia's southern flanks. Although access to natural reserves in the region was an important consideration, successive US administrations assessed the diplomatic costs to be too high to justify greater US engagement with the region. At the same time, a debate was raging within US academe on the relevance of Central Asia to US interests and the need for much more proactive policy towards the region. US scholars with links to policymaking circles, such as Paul Wolfowitz, Zbigniew Brzezinski and Frederick Starr, dismissed Russia's objections and the slow pace of reforms as determining factors in setting the agenda for US policy on Central Asia. This revisionist school of thought, which was closely associated with the Republican administration of President George W. Bush, was well placed in 2001 to take advantage of, and contribute to, the sudden shift in US foreign policy priorities.

The revisionist school's argument regarding the importance of Central Asia to US national security seemed to be vindicated when the United States decided to eliminate al-Qaeda in Afghanistan and remove the Taliban from power. The 'war on terror' also appeared to vindicate President Islam Karimov's earlier calls for an international campaign against the Taliban and Islamic insurgency in the region. This sudden shift in US policy, as will be analysed in Chapter 5, promised to make Uzbekistan a regional powerhouse and the main ally of the United States. Accordingly, Tashkent has reaffirmed its commitment to the United States and its international priorities. The most vivid example was during the US-led operation against Iraq in March 2003, when Uzbekistan stood out as the only Muslim state to offer wholehearted support for the US assault. Uzbek authorities ordered the local media to refrain from reproducing Russian coverage of the war, which was viewed as too critical of the United States.[6]

In contrast to expectations, closer ties between the United States and Uzbekistan and the positive influence of the former on the latter have not translated into greater political openness in this Central Asian state. There is no impetus for change. If anything, the Uzbek leadership feels even more vindicated and more confident that its domestic behaviour, however authoritarian, will not lead Washington to reassess fundamentally its relations with Uzbekistan. This belief explains, to a large extent, the Uzbek government's continued reluctance to heed calls for political openness. Chapter 6 explores this phase in US–Uzbek relations and the impact on domestic change, bearing in mind that issues of political reform and human rights have not been

Table 1 Uzbekistan's ethnic composition

	Uzbek	Tajik	Russian	Kazakh	Kyrgyz	Turkmen	Other	Total
million	19.23	1.4	1.15	1.05	0.21	0.16	1.94	25.15
%	76.5	5.5	4.6	4.2	0.9	0.6	7.7	100

Note: Population figures are based on the 1989 census and modified by natural growth rate and out-migration of Russians. Others include Tatars, Uighurs, Turks and Ukrainians.

Source: Olga Oliker and Thomas S. Szayna, eds, *Faultlines of Conflict in Central Asia: Implications for the U.S. Army* (Pittsburgh, PA: Rand Arroyo Centre, 2003), p. 157.

completely abandoned. Although they have lost their primacy in the US agenda, issues of human rights and democratic reforms are still covered by the US State Department factual reports on Uzbekistan, as well as by a host of non-governmental organisations. In response, Uzbek authorities have learned to behave deceptively, ordering an end to mass media censorship one day and sacking newspaper editors the next for publishing undesirable material.[7]

It is important to clarify here that the term 'Uzbek' in this book refers both to members of the Uzbek ethnic group and to citizens of Uzbekistan. It is, of course, obvious to any student of Central Asia that the five republics are ethnically heterogeneous. Ethnic Uzbeks in Uzbekistan constitute more than 75 per cent of the population. The rest of the population belong to other Central Asian nationalities, as well as Russians, Tatars and Ukrainians. Table 1 offers an estimated picture of the ethnic composition at the present time. So the use of the term 'Uzbek', instead of the cumbersome but politically correct label of 'Uzbekistani', is not intended to hide ethnic diversity. In the context on this study, however, the term 'Uzbek' is more relevant because (a) the leadership is almost exclusively Uzbek in its ethnic origins, and (b) its nationalist posturing is primarily aimed at the ethnic Uzbek majority in Uzbekistan. Consequently, the strict use of ethnic terminology is not deemed essential for the conceptual clarity of this study. In the occasional instances where ethnic differentiation is important to the discussion, for example the account of Tajiks' expulsion from their villages in Uzbekistan, the context makes that point clear.

Notes

1. Agence France Presse, 3 October 1996.
2. *Komsomol'skaya Pravda*, 6 October 1996.
3. *Nezavisimaya Gazeta*, 22 October 1996.
4. *Izvestia*, 12 August 1997.
5. As will be discussed in subsequent chapters, the Ferghana Valley has witnessed the greatest Islamic agitation in Uzbekistan. This seems to confirm a prediction by Donald S. Carlisle, who argued that 'The conventional wisdom that Tashkent has exaggerated the Islamic fundamentalist threat has some merit; but this should not lead to the facile conclusion that Karimov's fears are based on a mirage; Ferghana is in fact a boiling cauldron of economic and ethnic tensions ready to overflow at almost any time with terrible consequences for Uzbekistan, Tajikistan and especially Kyrgyzstan.' See Donald S. Carlisle, 'Geopolitics and Ethnic Problems of Uzbekistan and Its Neighbours', in Yaacov Ro'i, ed., *Muslim Eurasia: Conflicting Legacies* (Newbury Park: Frank Cass, 1995).
6. BBC Monitoring Central Asia Unit, 20 March 2003.
7. See the 2003 report on media restriction in Uzbekistan: Freedom House, *Freedom of the Press 2003* (Lanham, MD: Rowman & Littlefield, 2003), pp. 153–4.

I

From Soviet to Post-Soviet

Authoritarianism

The collapse of the Soviet Union in 1991 gave birth to new sovereign entities in Central Asia. Uzbekistan at the heart of that region tried to position itself quickly to take advantage of its new-found freedom. Tashkent took measures to establish relations with countries outside the Commonwealth of Independent States (CIS) and reformulate its relations with Russia on equal terms. But Tashkent's efforts to gain international recognition and attract diplomatic favour and financial investment were hampered by its poor record on political and economic reform and accountability. The United States and the European Union grew increasingly impatient with Tashkent for its failure to implement reforms. Despite the hype regarding transition to democracy, Uzbekistan appeared to be reverting to familiar patterns of authoritarianism within two years of the Soviet collapse. This reversal took place in the face of growing international concern and criticism, but proceeded nonetheless. The Uzbek leadership was determined not to be influenced by what it regarded as an impractical and utopian fascination with democracy and political openness. It rejected rapid transition or 'shock therapy' as risky and dangerous – a course to be avoided. Instead the Uzbek leadership prided itself on 'its own path', a jingoistic cover for no reforms.

Calls for political reforms by local opposition groups and the international community have focused on four main areas: freedom of association and the emergence and consolidation of a multiparty system; free and fair elections; freedom of information; and rule of law. Despite the engrained antipathy of the Uzbek leadership to the emergence of a competitive political system, these goals were nominally endorsed to placate international concerns. The record of political developments in the first decade of independence, however, provided little evidence to suggest that Uzbekistan was making progress on any of the above objectives. This should not come as a surprise since the leaders of independent Uzbekistan were former Soviet officials, trained and cultivated in an authoritarian system which sought to control every aspect of public life, and suspicious, even paranoid, about autonomous public activity. Contested elections in a multiparty system where the elected representatives are accountable to their electorate were anathema to the Soviet nomenklatura and its system of patronage. Democracy entailed potential risks of unpredictability and discontinuity for the leadership. Not surprisingly, Uzbek leaders chose to adopt 'democracy' in name only, building a façade of public accountability and choice while allowing as little as possible of these risky practices to infiltrate the post-Soviet state of Uzbekistan. In this, the Uzbek experience was far from unique. Perhaps with the notable exception of Turkmenistan, democracy has become the declaratory policy of all Central Asian states.

Leadership

President Islam Abduganivich Karimov is the most powerful man in Uzbekistan. His political career is typical of the current leadership. Islam Karimov was born in 1938 in Samarkand. A few years after obtaining his degree in economics and mechanical engineering, he started work with the republican Gosplan (state planning committee) in 1966. Karimov's political ascent started in 1983, when he enjoyed a sudden promotion to become the minister of finance. By late 1986 he was deputy chairman of the Council of Ministers and chairman of Gosplan. He was also selected first secretary of the Communist Party of the Kashkadar'ya regional committee in December 1986. In June 1989 Islam Karimov became first secretary of the Communist Party of Uzbekistan. And after the institutionalisation of the presidential system throughout the Soviet Union in March 1990, he was elected president by the republican parliament.[1]

The August putsch of 1991 was a test of President Karimov's conviction in Uzbekistan's future as a sovereign state outside the Soviet fold. He failed that test by his apparent indecision during the critical hours of the coup d'état which sought to turn back the clock and revive the disintegrating Soviet Union. On 20 August 1991, the state-controlled daily in Uzbekistan, *Pravda Vostoka*, published orders and public appeals issued by the coup plotters.[2] On the same day, at a joint meeting of the cabinet of ministers and the presidium of the Uzbek Supreme Soviet, the Uzbek leadership issued a mild criticism of the coup by deploring the use of force to settle 'political differences', but said nothing about the objectives of the coup. Instead Uzbek leaders appealed for calm, 'discipline and order'.[3] This episode did nothing for the nationalist credentials of Uzbek leaders, and they found it imperative to make corrective measures to avert a looming crisis of legitimacy.

Following the collapse of the attempted coup, which made independence for Uzbekistan inevitable, the Uzbek leadership sought to address the obvious shortcoming in its mandate to govern and its nationalist credentials. On 31 August 1991 the Supreme Soviet declared Uzbekistan an independent republic.[4] The Communist Party of Uzbekistan was suspended for its alleged links with coup plotters and on 17 September 1991 President Karimov issued a decree banning Communist Party activities in government organs.[5] This decree made no correlative impact on the composition of the personnel, who had originally gone through the nomenklatura vetting and selection process. The same leaders remained fully in control under the new banner of Uzbek nationalism. The renaming of the Communist Party of Uzbekistan to the People's Democratic Party of Uzbekistan (PDPU), on 1 November 1991,[6] helped this transition and allowed former Communist Party chiefs to stay in their government posts.

President Islam Karimov sought to keep a firm grip on the reigns of power and favoured the presidential system of government for the opportunities it offered.[7] The new Constitution, adopted in December 1992, contained extensive presidential powers. They included the power to:

- Appoint and dismiss the prime minister, his first deputy, deputy prime ministers, members of the cabinet of ministers, the procurator-general and his deputies, with subsequent confirmation by the parliament (Oliy Majlis).

- Nominate the chairman and members of the Constitutional Court, the Supreme Court, and the Higher Economic Court; and the chairman of the board of the Central Bank.
- Appoint and dismiss judges of regional, district, city and arbitration courts.
- Appoint and dismiss regional administrators (hakims) and for the city of Tashkent with subsequent confirmation by relevant regional and city councils (the president shall have the right to dismiss any hakim, should the latter violate the Constitution or the laws, or perform an act discrediting the honour and dignity of a hakim.
- Dissolve the Oliy Majlis (to be endorsed by the Constitutional Court) in case of insurmountable differences between the parliamentary deputies and the president.[8]

Of the above-mentioned presidential powers, the right to appoint regional hakims has proven to be an effective and reliable way to extend President Karimov's control and authority to local levels. The benefits of this mechanism are threefold. First, local hakims are answerable to the president and President Karimov has used this factor to consolidate his authority at the expense of competing interest groups within the political elite (see discussion on Shukrulla Mirsaidov below).[9] Hakims' loyalty and allegiance to President Karimov offer him a power base beyond the reach of parliamentary jurisdiction. The informal nature of personal relations and the emphasis on the president and the wisdom of his decisions reinforce the entrenched image of President Karimov as indispensable to Uzbekistan's future. It tends to blur the line between formal institutions of the state and the person of the president. The consequent cult of personality is a modern re-enactment of oriental despotism.

Second, President Karimov's rule is projected onto the local level through the hierarchical nature of regional and city administration. Hakims, as representatives of the president, have the authority to confirm or reject leaders at the level of neighbourhoods (*mahalla*). As a consequence, *aqsaqals* (literally 'whitebeards'), who are the respected elders of each locality, are incorporated into the political system. The *aqsaqal*, although elected by *mahalla* residents, depends on the endorsement of the city or regional hakim to assume the paid position of neighbourhood chief. This arrangement allows hakims to interfere in, and direct, *mahalla* affairs. The incorporation of the traditional, and hitherto informal, system of respect for the elders in the state structure is significant for President Karimov's claim to a popular mandate.[10] This is an important pillar of power. The *aqsaqal* plays an important role in the social life of his *mahalla* and performs various aspects of social security. The direct link to hakims and indirect connection to the president work in two important ways. They allow political management at micro-level and evoke an air of benevolence for President Karimov for his ultimate responsibility in upholding traditional Uzbek practices and the welfare of ordinary citizens.

Third, in a cyclic system of mutual reinforcement, hakims and their councils are allowed to nominate parliamentary candidates to the legislature (Oliy Majlis). In the 1999 parliamentary elections, 110 seats were won by local council candidates, including 75 provincial and city hakims.[11] Occupying nearly 45 per cent of the 250 seats in the Oliy Majlis, members of the executive branch at the local level, who are not required to forfeit their administrative office, constitute the single most powerful force in the legislative assembly. The consequent blurring of the line between the executive and the legislature gives President Karimov a significant degree of influence over the Oliy Majlis.

This brief account of the institutions of the state makes it clear that Uzbekistan's institutional hierarchy has been carefully crafted to privilege President Karimov. A revealing example of institutional fiddling to ensure total compliance with Karimov's wishes and to eliminate potential challenges was provided in 1992 when the office of vice-president was abolished.[12] Until its abolition, this office was held by Shukrulla Mirsaidov, an able political leader in his own right who did not always agree with Karimov's policies.[13] Mirsaidov was closely associated with Tashkent-based political leaders who regarded Karimov a political novice and his performance lacking in finesse. Mirsaidov was among 200 parliamentary deputies who signed an open letter in September 1991 criticising President Karimov's authoritarian tendencies. William Fierman, a long-time researcher on Uzbekistan, has argued that this episode suggested that Mirsaidov was preparing for a leadership challenge.[14] That is precisely how Islam Karimov interpreted the open letter initiative. It must have been clear to President Karimov that he would have to confront Mirsaidov and his allies if he wished to become the unopposed ruler of Uzbekistan. Disbanding the office of vice-president consolidated the president's position and gave him unrestrained control over the executive. President Karimov has been personally involved in the selection of the Cabinet of Ministers and moved to appoint loyal officials, often tied to Samarkand, to ministerial posts.[15] This arrangement rendered the office of the prime minister symbolic, devoid of real power, as openly admitted by former prime minister Abdulhashim Mutalov, who was removed from office in December 1995.[16]

President Karimov's power rests on a network of informal relations and loyalties, as well as formal institutions which allow the centralisation of power and merging of the executive and the legislative branches of the state. These two pillars of Karimov's authority are important for the continued functioning of his regime and the projected image of legitimacy, even popularity. For that reason, parliamentary and presidential elections are very important to the regime – not because they provide an opportunity for lawful transition, but because of their symbolism. They, invariably, reaffirm the image of popularity that the Uzbek leadership depends on to justify its rule. Constructing and maintaining the façade of a popular mandate is an ongoing project that is intended to address domestic and external critics. Tashkent insists that Uzbekistan has moved away from Soviet practices of sham elections where the ruling Communist Party nominated one candidate for each parliamentary seat. Both 1994 and 1999 parliamentary elections were contested by a number of political parties and multiple candidates. In the last elections, the PDPU won 48 seats, followed by Fidokorlar (34 seats) and Vatan Taraqiyoti (20 seats). Table 1.1 presents the election results in full.

The appearance of multiparty elections, however, cannot mask the fact that these were a highly elaborate exercise in delusion. None of the contesting parties had a platform that seemed even remotely different from the government's agenda. In 1995 Adolat (Justice) and Miliy Tiklanish (National Renaissance) were formed in response to criticism that Uzbekistan was not making progress towards a multi-party system.[17] This situation seems to confirm reports that President

Table 1.1 Parliamentary election results in 1994 and 1999 (number of seats won)

Electoral entities	1994	1999
People's Democratic Party of Uzbekistan	69	48
Vatan Taraqiyoti	14	20
Adolat	−	11
Millyi Tiklanish	−	10
Fidokorlar	−	34
Local authorities	167	110
Initiative groups	−	16
Total	250	249

Source: EurasiaNet Election Monitor.

Karimov regarded the emergence of public organisations and political parties as a sign of anarchy – that is, the failure of state authority.[18] But political expediency forced the leadership to retract these explicitly anti-democratic propositions and allow a semblance of a multiparty system. In January 1999 a new party was registered, just in time for the coming parliamentary polls. Fidokorlar (Self-sacrificers) declared its loyalty to President Karimov and his policies at its inaugural meeting and, in the following year, nominated him for re-election at the 2000 presidential elections.[19] The proliferation of political parties in the mid- to late 1990s helped move the political system away from the dichotomous model of ruling party versus loyal opposition. President Karimov helped accelerate this process by resigning as head of the PDPU in 1996, which allowed him to preside above and beyond party politics. The sharp drop in the PDPU's parliamentary seats at the last elections indicated the extent of this shift. The spread of the popular vote for registered parties, all of which have publicly declared allegiance to President Karimov, suggest that political parties are, in effect, irrelevant to Uzbekistan. Despite this, these parties have an important public-relations role to play and will continue to be visible on the political scene. In April 2000 Fidokorlar incorporated Vatan Taraqiyoti, leading to its emergence as the largest party bloc in the Oliy Majlis. The next parliamentary elections, scheduled for December 2004, are likely to continue this trend and witness further erosion in the number of seats held by the PDPU.

A constant feature of politics in Uzbekistan is the primary role of President Karimov. Even though the post-Soviet Constitution does not allow a person to serve more than two consecutive terms, President Karimov looks set to remain in presidential office for well over fifteen years. Following his election by the parliament in March 1990, Islam Karimov sought a popular mandate and won the first direct presidential elections in the history of Uzbekistan in December 1991. He defeated Muhammad Solih, leader of Erk, the opposition party, by a convincing margin: 86 to 14 per cent. Karimov's five-year term was to expire in 1996, but a referendum in March of that year extended his presidency until 2000. This extension allowed him to stand for elections for a second consecutive term. In January 2000 President Karimov was re-elected with over 90 per cent of the votes. His opponent, Abdulhafez Jalalov, first secretary of the PDPU, received less than 5 per cent of the votes, and was quoted as admitting that he voted for Islam Karimov.[20] Following the launch of the 'war on terror' and Uzbekistan's new-found importance in the US security operations in the region, President Karimov sought to consolidate his position even further and orchestrated another referendum to extend his term to seven years. The results of the January 2002 referendum were not surprising; Karimov's term was extended to 2007. This performance confirmed critical assessments that Islam Karimov has no intention of leaving office. Incidentally, the speaker of the Oliy Majlis, Erkin Khalilov, had indeed suggested that Islam Karimov should be made president for life before the 2002 referendum.[21] It is interesting to note that the close relationship between Tashkent and Washington that emerged in the post-September 11 era appeared to have no visible impact on the behaviour of the leadership in Uzbekistan.

All post-Soviet elections and referendums have been criticised by international observers as fraught with irregularities and falling short of acceptable standards for 'free and fair' elections. The December 1991 presidential elections were perhaps the most open public contest, taking place in an atmosphere of optimism. By 1990, the gradual withdrawal of Moscow from Central Asian affairs had provided for certain openings in the political sphere. Two secular political parties led the movement for Uzbek national assertiveness at the time: the Birlik Popular movement and the Erk Democratic Party. These parties held an ambiguous position on the question of secession from the Soviet Union. While highly critical of Moscow for its exploitation of Uzbek resources and the environmental disaster caused by the Soviet-imposed cotton monoculture, they refrained from calling for a clean break with the Soviet Union. Instead they confined themselves, by and large, to propagating the promotion of Uzbek language and culture. They were critical of the Communist Party leadership, at the time under Islam Karimov's first secretariatship, for its failure to uphold Uzbek identity in the face of the ongoing Russianisation of the public sphere.[22]

The restoration of Uzbek as the official language of the state, therefore, became the galvanising motif. Cultural assertiveness became a conduit for political expression. For example, an opposition rally in Tashkent was ordained with banners which read something like 'He Who Abandons His Mother Tongue Will Abandon His People'.[23] This was a not-so-subtle attack on the republican Communist Party leadership for failing to uphold Uzbek identity, led by the Uzbek intelligentsia. In this context Muhammad Solih, leader of Erk, had the right credentials to be at the forefront of the campaign for the 'Uzbekisation' of the state. As the secretary of Uzbekistan's Writers' Union, Mohammad Solih had long been a champion of cultural revival.[24]

The social base of Erk and Birlik among the intelligentsia made them a potent force. This made President Karimov sensitive to the challenge they could pose and informed his decision to disarm them through adopting the same nationalist agenda. President Karimov's electoral platform of 1991 had the same emphasis on the 'spiritual revival of the nation' that was espoused by Muhammad Solih.[25] Underlining the supposedly unique nature of Uzbekistan's experience, President Karimov delivered a series of lectures on the 'Uzbek way' to independent state-building.[26]

Yet the adoption of the opposition's nationalist programme did not translate into tolerating these parties. While the opposition was busy organising rallies and holding public meetings, the Karimov regime was busy adopting a series of new laws to prepare the legal basis for curbing any activity deemed to be harmful to 'national unity' and order in Uzbekistan. William Fierman recounts the adoption of these laws as significant in reining in autonomous political activity. These included the Law on Protecting the Honour and Dignity of the President (adopted in February 1991), the Law on Public Associations in the Uzbek SSR (adopted in February 1991), the Law on Mass Media (adopted in June 1991), and the Law on Freedom of Conscience and Religious Organisation (adopted in June 1991).[27] They placed strict limitations on opposition groups, barring them from receiving funds from international sources, using the state-controlled media to deliver their message, which was deemed to propagate ethnic or religious exclusivity, or undermine the moral foundations of society. After months of harassment and attacks on their leaders, Erk and Birlik were banned in 1993 and charged with conspiracy to overthrow the elected government. Many opposition activists were imprisoned for 'defaming the honour of President Karimov'.[28]

An important dimension of the curb on opposition activity related to Islamic political initiatives. Political Islam, a movement to remould political institutions (primarily the state) in accordance with principles of Islam, was a novel phenomenon in Uzbekistan. In 1991, Uzbekistan witnessed the emergence of political Islam in an embryonic form: the Islamic Renaissance Party (IRP) tried to hold its founding congress in January 1991, leading to the arrest and detention of its leaders.[29] The above-mentioned law on public associations prohibited the formation of political parties based on religion.[30] The same prohibition was adopted earlier in neighbouring Tajikistan to curb the growth of IRP's sister organisation in that republic.[31]

In spite of these restrictions, the IRP continued to attract a following and mobilise mass protests in conjunction with Birlik and Erk. As will be discussed in the following chapter, the IRP's platform was vague and imprecise. In October 1992, the party's leader, Haji Abdullah Utaev (Uta Ogly), surrounded by IRP activists, argued for the Islamisation of the state and the adoption of the sharia as the guiding principle of the Constitution. But he rejected revolution as unsuitable and undesirable for achieving that objective. Uzbekistan, he stated, was not Iran, and the ideal Islamic state would not violate the rights of religious and ethnic minorities. Beyond these general proclamations, Utaev could not elaborate on the operational format of the ideal Islamic state.[32] One point was clear: the Soviet system had removed Islam from the public domain and it was important to redress this alien practice. This desire to restore Islam's relevance to public life and the aversion to detailing the projected goal characterised all IRP pamphlets and publications. This lack of ideological clarity, and the practical record of the IRP's activity in association with the secular-minded organisations of Erk and Birlik, point to a different picture than the simplistic one portrayed by the regime. It may be argued that the IRP was yet another Uzbek nationalist organisation, one with greater attachment to pre-Soviet traditions and committed to reversing the Soviet aberration in the history of Uzbeks. Whatever the underlying motifs of the IRP, it was promptly eliminated from the political scene through a combination of harassment, persecution and prosecution. Soon after the 1992 interview, Utaev disappeared, generally believed to have been abducted by security forces.[33]

Islam

Tashkent's response to the IRP and relations with Islam was problematic. The political elite in Uzbekistan was imbued with the Soviet mistrust of religion. President Karimov's leadership was not prepared to tolerate political mobilisation by an Islamic party. At the same time, the leadership was desperate for legitimacy and public acceptance. It had adopted the mantle of nationalism by way of disarming the opposition, and in that process the leadership could not ignore the emotional attachment of Uzbeks to Islam. President Karimov conceded that Islam was an important part of Uzbek heritage and a central pillar of national identity. That was an important factor that contributed to the failure of Soviet efforts to eradicate Islam. The leadership understood that its nation-building enterprise would be incomplete without due attention to Islam and its role in Independent Uzbekistan. It, therefore, tried to align itself with the Islamic revival that was sweeping through the country.[34]

As argued by Yaacov Ro'i, the Islamic revival was a manifestation of national pride and assertiveness.[35] The Uzbek leadership understood this. Political expediency explains the respectful tone of President Karimov on Islam on the eve of the December 1991 elections. In

an interview with the Uzbek language daily *Khalq Sozi*, he insisted
that Islam was at the heart of the Uzbek way of life: 'Islam is the
conscience, the essence of life, the very life of our countrymen.'[36]
President Karimov continued his championship of Islam in the heady
days of 1992, immediately after the Soviet collapse. His government
sponsored religious celebrations and designated *Qurban bairam* (*'id
al-qurban*) and *Uruza bairam* (*'id al-Fitr*) as national holidays.[37] In subsequent years President Karimov consistently called on hakims and
local government apparatuses to organise these Islamic feasts.

The Karimov leadership openly identified itself with the Islamic
heritage of the region and, in that process, helped merge national
and Islamic identities. For example, in a parliamentary speech in
September 1994, President Karimov identified Islamic thinkers such
as Muhammad al-Bukhari, Muhammad Ali al-Termezi and Khoja
Bahoutdin Naqshband as the great ancestors of modern-day Uzbeks.[38]
In the same month the Uzbek government organised an anniversary
celebration of Bahoutdin Naqshband's birthday, and the official press
referred to the founder of Naqshbandi Sufism as 'our great ancestor
and torch-bearer of theological science'.[39] Similar nationalist honour
was bestowed on Muhammad al-Bukhari at an international conference in Tashkent.[40]

In the same vein, President Karimov had been consistent in
manufacturing for himself an image of piety and benevolence. He
has repeatedly incorporated references to 'Allah's wishes' in his
public speeches and places his hand on the Koran at his presidential
inauguration ceremonies (1992 and 2000). These public displays
of reverence for Islam have won President Karimov some support
– most significantly from the Mufti of Tashkent, Mukhtarjon Abdullah
al-Bukhari, who believes Islam Karimov lives up to his name. The
mufti argues that President Karimov prays regularly and 'submits to
the will of Allah'.[41] This overwhelming endorsement from the chief
Islamic authority in Uzbekistan, however, masks a difficult relationship between the government and the office of the muftiyat in the
aftermath of the Soviet collapse.

The leadership's Soviet training taught them to keep a tight lid
on social/political activity; Islam was not immune from that. From
the very first days of independence the authorities tried to reassert
control over the office of the muftiyat through the Soviet-constructed

State Committee for Religious Affairs.[42] Under the energetic leadership of Mufti Muhammad Sadiq Muhammad Yusuf, the muftiyat was evolving from a subservient body into a more independent organisation with its own interests. In the 1991–92 period the muftiyat was actively lobbying for more freedom of religious expression, Islamic education and training for unregistered imams/prayer leaders. Mufti Muhammad Yusuf was also a close friend of the Tajik Qazi-kalon Akbar Turajonzoda, who was by mid-1992 embroiled in the Tajik civil war. Although Mufti Muhammad Yusuf did not adopt a confrontational approach in relation to Uzbek authorities, it was clear to the leadership that the muftiyat's growing autonomy from the state might not be reversed while Muhammad Yusuf remained in office. Consequently, Mufti Muhammad Yusuf was removed from the highest office of Islamic jurisprudence in Uzbekistan in April 1993.[43] His replacement, Imam Mukhtarjon Abdullah al-Bukhari,[44] had a very different personality. More a scholar of Islam than an advocate, Mufti Abdullah has been described by some members of the muftiyat as too weak and 'subservient' to hold the position. But so far as the authorities were concerned, these very qualities must have made him the perfect candidate.

The authorities' success in bringing the muftiyat under strict state control and reversing its social activism of the early 1990s was an important link in the chain of events that led to the consolidation of post-Soviet authoritarianism in Uzbekistan. In a way, the subjugation of the muftiyat was more difficult than banning opposition parties. Mufti Muhammad Yusuf was widely respected as a scholar and voice of moderation, quite conscious of the government's priorities and constraints as well as the strength of pacifist Islam in Uzbek society. He did not shy away from rejecting Islamic radicalism and the IRP as alien to Uzbeks. When asked about his views on the formation of the IRP, he flatly rejected the move as divisive and ill-conceived.[45]

For that reason, the government had to move tactfully and present his removal as an internal matter for the ulema. This allowed the regime to maintain its elaborate promotion of Islamic traditions and beliefs, while emasculating it of any political force.

Immediately after the Soviet collapse, the political atmosphere was filled with expectations and hope for a free Uzbekistan. But every day that passed the leadership moved a step further in the path of reconstructing the authoritarian state. In contrast with the Soviet precedent, the state did not replicate an alien model and a foreign ideology. Instead it portrayed itself as representing indigenous traditions and upholding public good and social stability. The curbs against freedom of expression and association were justified in terms of the need for order and unity. Images of Islamic militancy played a central role in this scenario as extremism was blamed for threatening everything that was good in Uzbekistan. Strict measures and heightened state control over the public domain were presented as a small price to pay for the protection of the national way of life. This line of argument was rejected by international agencies and the United States in the first decade of Uzbekistan's independence. But, as will be discussed in the following chapters, the force of international criticism of Uzbekistan's record of authoritarian reversion has subsided in the aftermath of September 11.

Notes

1. Biography extracted from *Pravda Vostoka*, 30 November 1991.
2. *Pravda Vostoka*, 20 August 1991, p. 1.
3. *Pravda Vostoka*, 21 August 1991, p. 1.
4. *Pravda Vostoka*, 1 September 1991, p. 1.
5. See 'Ukaz o departizatsii organov gosudarsatvennei vlasti i upravleneniya i sistemy narodnogo obrazovaniya respubliki', in *Pravda Vostoka*, 18 September 1991. It is interesting to note that the Russian president, Boris Yeltsin, had issued a similar decree two months earlier.
6. *Pravda Vostoka*, 2 November 1991.
7. For a fascinating assessment of the elite's perception of political reforms and implications for transition from the Soviet model of government, see Pauline Jones Luong, *Institutional Change and Political Continuity in Post-Soviet Central Asia* (Cambridge: Cambridge University Press, 2002). There is a large literature on 'super-presidentialism' in the post-Soviet space. It is, however, not appropriate to adopt this concept for the political system in Uzbekistan, in place of authoritarianism. Super-presidentialism allows for contested elections and electoral challenges to the incumbent. Adopting this concept would ignore Uzbekistan's record of political intolerance and blur differences between this Central Asian state and Russia, where civil society and political dissent have been accepted, if grudgingly, as part of the political process. For Russia-focused studies, see Timothy J. Colton, 'Superpresidentialism and Russia's Backwater State', *Post-Soviet Affairs*, vol. 11, no. 2, 1995, pp. 144–8, and M. Steven Fish, 'The Executive Deception: Superpresidentialism and the Degradation of

Russian Politics', in Valerie Sperling, ed., *Building the Russian State: Institutional Crisis and the Quest for Democratic Governance* (Boulder, CO: Westview Press, 2000). For an unconvincing attempt to extend the concept of super-presidentialism to other states in the CIS, see John T. Ishiyama and Ryan Kennedy, 'Superpresidentialism and Political party Development in Russia, Ukraine, Armenia and Kyrgyzstan', *Europe–Asia Studies*, vol. 53, no. 8, 2001, pp. 1177–91.

8. *Constitution of the Republic of Uzbekistan*, www.umid.uz/Main/Uzbekistan/Constitution; see Appendix A.

9. For an informative assessment of regional divisions within the elite, see Donald Carlisle, 'The Uzbek Power Elite: Politburo and the Secretariat (1938–83)', *Central Asia Survey*, vol. 5, no. 3–4, 1986, pp. 91–132. There is very little in the public domain to help researchers ascertain the extent and relevance of regional factionalism in Uzbekistan, but a recent report in the Russian media suggested that such divisions continue to persist. See Vladimir Muhin, Marina Kozhushko and Tat'iana Rybleva, 'V Uzbekistane "pokhornili" presidenta – Tashkentskie clany delyat vlast' – opirayas' na slukhi o smerti Islama Karimova', *Nezavisimaya Gazeta*, 6 March 2003.

10. Olivier Roy has labelled this process the 'indigenisation' of the state, which tends to stifle autonomous social activity at the local level by institutionalising the leading role of the *aqsaqal*. Olivier Roy, *The New Central Asia, the Creation of Nations* (London: I.B. Tauris, 2000), pp. 182–3.

11. EurasiaNet Election Monitor, www.eurasianet.org/departments/election/uzbekistan/uzelup0300.html.

12. *Nezavisimaya Gazeta*, 16 January 1992.

13. RFE/RL, *Daily Report*, 9 January 1992.

14. William Fierman, 'Political Development in Uzbekistan: Democratization?', in Karen Dawisha and Bruce Parrott, eds, *Conflict, Cleavage and Change in Central Asia and the Caucasus* (Cambridge: Cambridge University Press, 1997), p. 378.

15. Communication with the exiled politician Babur Malikov, former Minister of Justice in Uzbekistan, 27 February 1995.

16. *Nezavisimaya Gazeta*, 27 December 1995.

17. For a highly critical account of party formation in Uzbekistan, see Abdumannob Polat, 'New Karimov-Organized Political Party in Uzbekistan', 30 December 1998, available on www.birlik.net/fidokor.htm.

18. Fierman, 'Political Development in Uzbekistan', p. 373.

19. Organization of Security and Cooperation in Europe – Office for Democratic Institutions and Human Rights, *Republic of Uzbekistan. Election of Deputies to the Oliy Majlis (Parliament)*, 5 & 19 December 1999, available at www.osce.org/odihr/documents/reports/election_reports/uz/uzb00–1–final.pdf.

20. RFE/RL, *NewsLine*, 11 January 2000.

21. Joshua Machleder, 'Confusion and Cynicism Mark Uzbek Referendum', *EurasiaNet.Org*, 1/28/02, www.eurasianet.org/departments/insight/articles/eavo12802.shtml.

22. For a detailed and informative account of the emergence of Uzbek nationalism, especially on the eve of independence, see James Critchlow, *Nationalism in Uzbekistan: A Soviet Republic's Road to Sovereignty* (Boulder, CO: Westview Press, 1991).

23. Timur Kocaoglu, "Demonstrations by Uzbek Popular Front", *Report on the USSR*, 28 April 1989, p. 14.

24. Annette Bohr, 'Restoring the Uzbek Cultural Heritage: Uzbek Literary Journal Proposes Study of Ancient Turkic Script', RFE/RL *Research Report*, 5 December 1988.

25. Solih's programme appeared in *PravdaVostoka*, 10 December 1991. President Karimov responded by giving an interview and covering all aspects of the Erk programme under the heading 'our own path'. See *Pravda Vostoka*, 20 December 1991.

26. Jacob M. Landau and Barbara Kellner-Heinkele present a comprehensive account of the Uzbek government's adoption of the nationalist demands in relation to Uzbek language, within the broad context of emerging language nationalism in Central Asia. See Jacob M. Landau and Barbara Kellner-Heinkele, *Politics of Language in the ex-Soviet Muslim States* (London: C. Hurst, 2001).

27. Fierman, 'Political Development in Uzbekistan', pp. 375–7.

28. RFE/RL *Daily Report*, 7 March 1994.

29. *Pravda Vostoka*, 1 February 1991.

30. See text of 'Ob obshchestvennykh ob'edineniyakh v Uzbekskoi SSR', in *Pravda Vostoka*, 26 February 1991.

31. See text of 'Zakon Tadzhikskoi sovetskoi sotsialisticheskoi respubliki ob obshchestvennykh ob'edineniyakh v Tadzhikskoi SSR', in *Kommunist Tadzhikistana*, 28 December 1990.

32. Interview with Haji Abdullah Utaev (Uta Ogly), leader of the IRP, Tashkent, 10 October 1992.

33. See Bureau of Democracy, Human Rights, and Labor, US Department of State, *Uzbekistan. Country Report on Human Rights Practices for 1997*, 30 January 1998, www.usis.usemb.se/human/human97/uzbekist.html.

34. The best example of this revival is the growth of mosques in the latter part of the 1980s and the first half of the 1990s. According to Alexandre Bennigsen and Enders Wimbush, in 1982 there were only 150 registered mosques in Uzbekistan; by 1989 William Fierman records 170 registered mosques and 250 by 1990. According to my interviews with officials from the muftiyat in August 1995, this number had then reached 5,000. See Alexandre Bennigsen and Enders S. Wimbush, *Mystics and Commissars* (Berkeley, CA: University of California Press, 1985), p. 153; William Fierman, 'Policy toward Islam in Uzbekistan in the Gorbachev era', *Nationalities Papers*, vol. 22, no. 1, 1994, p. 234.

35. Yaacov Ro'i, 'The Secularization of Islam and the USSR's Muslim Areas', in Yaacov Ro'i, ed., *Muslim Eurasia: Conflicting Legacies* (Newbury Park: Frank Cass, 1995), p. 12.

36. Reproduced in the Russian-language daily *Pravda Vostoka*, 20 December 1991.

37. See 'Zakon o prazdnichnykh dnyakh v respubliki Uzbekistan', *Pravda Vostoka*, 16 July 1992, p. 1.
38. *Pravda Vostoka*, 24 September 1994, p. 1.
39. *Pravda Vostoka*, 17 September 1994, p. 2.
40. *Pravda Vostoka*, 20 September 1994, p. 2.
41. Interview with Mufti Mukhtarjon Abdullah al-Bukhari, Tashkent, 6 July 1995.
42. For an extensive account, see Shahram Akbarzadeh, 'Islamic Clerical Establishment In Central Asia', *South Asia*, vol. 20, no. 2, December 1997, pp. 73–102.
43. *Nezavisimaya Gazeta*, 28 April 1993.
44. RFE/RL, *Daily Reports*, 3 May 1993.
45. *Komsomol'skaya Pravda*, 8 December 1990, p. 1.

2

Islamic Challenge

The Uzbek regime's relations with Islam followed a complex and contradictory course. The pattern was set in the first few years of independence. Events such as the civil war in neighbouring Tajikistan (1992–97) and the American campaign against Islamic terrorism in the region (2001–present) have added to the complexity of Islam–regime relations. On the one hand, following the Soviet collapse the regime needed to enhance its legitimacy and distance itself from its past. It was hoped that adopting the mantle of nationalism would achieve that. The leadership was fully aware of the importance of Islam in Uzbek self-identification and that no nationalist programme would be complete without a salient Islamic component. President Islam Karimov made explicit gestures to show his loyalty and deference to Islam, and made repeated claims about the importance of Islamic thinkers to the spiritual well-being of Uzbeks, as indicated in the previous chapter. On the other hand, the Uzbek leadership insisted on a formal separation of Islam from politics and viewed with grave suspicion attempts to politicise Islam in any way beyond the prescribed framework of endorsing government policies. The ingrained fear of political Islam, which was labelled 'fundamentalist' or 'Wahhabi', put the regime at loggerheads with autonomous political actors with an Islamic orientation. The increasingly repressive measures taken against Islamic groups and organisations were justified in terms of national security and political stability. The Tajik civil war, the Tashkent bombings in 1999, armed incursions into Kyrgyz and Uzbek territories by the Islamic Movement of Uzbekistan in 1999, 2000 and 2001, and the shocking attack on the World Trade Center on 11 September 2001 have served as evidence of the threat. So far as Tashkent is concerned, these examples vindicate the Uzbek government's warnings of Islamic extremism.

Yet the history of Islamic activism in Uzbekistan does not support the official presentation of Islamic radicalism as an ever-present danger, requiring constant vigilance. This chapter will explore the emergence and the gradual radicalisation of Islamic activism in the post-Soviet decade. It traces the transformation of loosely organised autonomous Islamic groups into militant clandestine organisations. The evolution of political Islam from a movement for reform into an uncompromising force for political change points to the open-ended nature of Islam in Uzbekistan. It is also important to take note of external factors that have contributed to the radicalisation of political Islam. This chapter will, therefore, conclude with an examination of the growing role of Hizb ut-Tahrir (Liberation Party).

Emerging Islamism

The formation of the Islamic Renaissance Party (IRP) of Uzbekistan in January 1991 was the first attempt to build a political platform on Islamic foundations. But the IRP proved ill-prepared for the task. This was evident in its organisational structure and ideological/political framework. From its inception, the IRP under the leadership of Abdullah Utaev (Uta Ogly) carried strong nationalist tendencies. This was evident in the fact that even though it was formed as part of a larger Soviet-wide organisation, which was launched in Russia (in Astrakhan) the previous year, the IRP operated autonomously. The unexpected collapse of the Soviet Union and Uzbekistan's independence in December 1991 helped consolidate the IRP's autonomy from its sister organisations in Russia and neighbouring Central Asian states. It is noteworthy that not even the long history of close ties between Uzbeks and Tajiks could facilitate better coordination between their respective organisations. The onset of civil war in Tajikistan in May 1992 acted as a wedge to separate them even further. While Utaev and his cohorts shared with their Tajik counterparts the desire to promote Islamic order, albeit ill-defined, and the ultimate goal of establishing an Islamic state, they distanced themselves from the militant tactics used in Tajikistan and refrained from getting involved in the Tajik civil war.

Politically, the IRP maintained ambiguous and, at times, contradictory goals. As a general rule, the rallying cry of all Islamist groups has been 'social justice', and the formation of an Islamic state to achieve that. The IRP in Uzbekistan was no exception to the rule and favoured an alternative to the political corruption of communism and the moral and social decadence of capitalism to achieve social justice.[1] But some important questions remained unanswered in the IRP platform. For example, it was far from clear how the projected Islamic polity would operate and guarantee social justice. Would the borders of this Islamic state be demarcated along the existing boundaries? What tools were legitimate in the pursuit of this objective? The IRP's often contradictory position on these issues undermined its popular appeal.

As an Islamic party committed to the ideal of Islamic community (umma), the IRP could not reject the notion of a transnational Islamic unity. But this desire was tempered on two levels. The first was a sense that Uzbek Muslims had much more in common with their Central Asian neighbours than with other Muslims to the south. A nostalgic interpretation of history, popular among many young Uzbeks and activists in the IRP following the Soviet collapse, glorified an imaginary era of unity in Central Asia or Turkestan, as it was known before the tsarist colonisation in the second half of the nineteenth century. IRP activists intuitively favoured a unitary Islamic system that covered all, or most, of Central Asia regardless of ethnic differences. This tendency highlighted the first contradiction between the limitless ideal of umma and the geographically confined (and historically familiar) notion of an Islamic Turkestan. This contradiction was compounded by a further limitation on the ideal umma, this time on nationalist grounds. It was revealing that the IRP leadership refrained from advocating a transnational alternative, even at its height in the first half of 1992, instead limiting itself to Uzbek territory as the arena for its activities.

The IRP leadership's choice revealed an important feature in the political psychology of the Uzbek intelligentsia (intellectuals, cultural and social leaders and commentators, including religious scholars), and more specifically in the nature of the IRP. Forgoing the grand all-encompassing vision of *umma* for the rather small Islamic Uzbekistan exhibited the extent to which the idea of Uzbek national distinctness, or *Uzbekchilik*, had gained acceptance among secular and Islamic intellectuals and leaders. The novel Uzbek national identity, created under the systematic Soviet policy on nationalities, had now captured the imagination of the intelligentsia and demarcated the contours of their political activity.

In spite of an instinctive desire to transcend national boundaries, the IRP leadership steered a pragmatic course and kept its transnational impulses in check. This was evident in a number of revealing cases. Foremost was its abstention from siding with its sister organisation in Tajikistan in 1992. Following the same pattern, the IRP showed no interest in the rest of the Muslim world except Afghanistan.[2] The IRP's attitude to Afghanistan was determined by a mixture of pragmatism and ideology. The IRP's leadership was visibly heartened by the victory of the Afghan mujahidin to expel Soviet forces in 1989. The Afghan victory was of special interest to the IRP, not only because the two states shared a border but also because ethnic Uzbeks in Afghanistan were among the victors. This made the Afghan experience highly relevant to Uzbekistan and the IRP leadership was keen to highlight the success of their compatriots. Prospects of an Islamic state in Afghanistan inspired the IRP. But, at the same time, the IRP was increasingly concerned with infighting among the Afghan mujahidin and Afghanistan's descent into anarchy. Consequently, Utaev was forced to maintain a difficult position on Afghanistan: praising the Afghan mujahidin in their jihad against Soviet infidels and in their attempt to build an Islamic state, while rejecting their factional rivalry which had resulted in disorder and civil war. It was imperative for the IRP to distance itself from the increasingly disastrous Afghan experience – but its conditional support for the Afghan mujahidin proved to be its Achilles heel as the IRP's vision was systematically compared with the Afghan calamity in Uzbekistan's state-controlled media.

In contrast the Islamic Revolution of Iran and the subsequent imposition of Islamic rule on society epitomised everything that the IRP leadership was desperate to reject. Utaev put it simply: 'the IRP does not follow the Iranian model'. Rejecting this 'undemocratic' model was an important measure in the IRP's attempt to gain legitimacy as a political force in 1991–92. Added to this pragmatic consideration was the IRP's distrust of Iranian Shia doctrine and practice, which were rejected as alien to Sunni Uzbeks.

Another important factor that revealed the IRP's nationalist orientation was its close collaboration with the secular/nationalist Birlik, and to a certain degree the more fiercely secular Erk. The leadership of Birlik and the IRP worked closely together in their campaign against the regime of President Islam Karimov, neither party allowing ideology to hamper their cooperation. This was made possible by the common understanding that genuine Uzbek sovereignty would have to reflect Uzbeks' affiliation with Islam. Birlik, while not promoting an Islamic vision for Uzbekistan, was quite open to incorporating aspects of Islam in a nationalist state. On the other hand, the IRP leadership had to admit that the ideal of Islamic rule in Uzbekistan could only be achieved if the state were governed by nationalist principles. Only a quintessential Uzbek state that allowed and encouraged expressions of Uzbek pride could facilitate the promotion of Islam, which it considered to be the cornerstone of Uzbek identity and heritage.

The salient nationalist flavour in the IRP message blurred the line between that organisation and the less avowedly religious alternatives. This ambiguity reflected the failure of the IRP to formulate a comprehensive and coherent political programme. As a consequence the IRP rank and file were left politically ill-equipped to respond to the propaganda campaign against the party rationale and objectives, orchestrated by President Karimov's regime.

Despite grand hopes and motivations, the IRP was unable to launch a serious challenge to the regime. It lacked long-term strategy, clarity of tactics and organisational skill to withstand the combined political and extrajudicial assault mounted by the regime in 1992 and 1993. It even failed to gain the approval of the influential Mufti Muhammad Yusuf, which seriously undermined the IRP's Islamic credentials in the eyes of many Uzbeks.[3] In short, the IRP was unable to present a serious challenge to the regime and disappeared after a short spate of activity in 1991–92. The Uzbek regime responded to the formation of the IRP by adopting (in February 1991) a new law on public organisations which banned religiously inspired political parties.[4] The IRP continued its activity illegally and hoped to annul this law in the wake of the Soviet collapse with support from Birlik, but to no avail. After enduring months of state-run propaganda, judicial prosecution and extrajudicial persecution, the turning point came with the suspicious case of Utaev's disappearance. The IRP never recovered from that blow. The so-called 'Islamic threat' which the regime maintained was imminent did not materialise.

For nearly five years the regime seemed to have overcome its feared, albeit exaggerated, Islamic challengers. The IRP was dispersed in 1993, and in neighbouring Tajikistan the anti-Islamist government of Emomali Rahmonov, with active support from Russia, was making gradual gains against the coalition of Islamic/democratic forces. If Tashkent's justifications for its authoritarian measures against the media, and society as a whole, are taken at face value, these internal and external developments should have resulted in the easing of government restrictions on autonomous political activity and expression of dissent. But the Uzbek regime used its success in relation to the IRP as a stepping stone to eliminate all forms of political autonomy (religious or secular). Birlik and Erk soon suffered the same fate, as did Mufti Muhammad Yusuf, who, despite his reluctance to become involved in politics, had antagonised the regime by guarding his office and the official Islamic establishment against government interference.[5]

Resurgence of Islamic Radicalism

In February 1999 Tashkent was rocked by a series of coordinated bombings, which were immediately blamed on the Islamic Movement of Uzbekistan (IMU). In the subsequent months, this little known organisation and its military commander Juma Namangani became familiar names in Central Asia. In August 1999 IMU fighters conducted a daring raid into the Batken district of Kyrgyzstan, close to the borders of Uzbekistan, and took village officials, residents and four Japanese scientists hostage.[6] The IMU declared this operation to be a tactical move against President Karimov's regime in Uzbekistan and not intended to destabilise Kyrgyzstan. The IMU demanded the release of political prisoners in Uzbekistan and a ransom. Unofficial reports suggest that Japan secretly paid over US$2 million to the IMU through Kyrgyz negotiators. All hostages were released in October, some five weeks after their capture, and the IMU used mountain tracks to pull back its guerrillas across the border into its camp in Tajikistan. Much to the frustration of the Kyrgyz and Uzbek security forces, the IMU repeated its armed forays in August 2000 and July 2001, at one point infiltrating Uzbek territory and engaging Uzbek security forces in the mountains just outside Tashkent.

The IMU was proving to be a much more agile and challenging force than its predecessor, the IRP. It demonstrated a remarkable ability to maintain an organised fighting force with sufficient funds and logistics to support its campaigns. This degree of sophistication was a result of its long formative experience in Afghanistan and the combined roles of two men from the city of Namangan in the Uzbekistani-controlled parts of the Ferghana Valley: Juma Namangani and Tahir Yuldosh.

Juma Namangani (real name Juma Khojaev) and Tahir Yuldosh were in their early twenties when Soviet troops were forced out of Afghanistan and Soviet power started to weaken. Namangani had served in Afghanistan as a Soviet army conscript and had developed profound respect for the Afghan mujahidin. He had also developed tactical military skills, which were later put to effective use in IMU's 1999–2001 campaigns. Namangani's charismatic and daring qualities were complemented by the Islamic knowledge and commitment of Tahir Yuldosh, a young unofficial mullah. Faced with a collapsing Soviet empire, Namangani and Yuldosh moved to assert their Islamic identity by building a Saudi-funded mosque in 1990. Events moved quickly in Namangan as the city mayor refused construction permission for the new mosque, enraging Yuldosh and his supporters (mostly unemployed youth). In December 1990, Uzbek youth seized the city office of the Communist Party of Uzbekistan, offering Yuldosh an unprecedented opportunity to implement his ideas. Neighbourhood watch committees were set up and a de facto Islamic order was initiated in Namangan, as women were encouraged to wear the hijab.

At the time Yuldosh was leading the Adolat (Justice) party, which had branches throughout Uzbekistan's Ferghana Valley. Adolat acted as the political training camp for young recruits who sought avenues of self-expression and Islamic assertion. The call for an Islamic state and the implementation of the sharia had particular appeal to this constituency. This was due to at least three interrelated factors: (1) the call for the supremacy of the sharia had a nostalgic ring, as it was widely believed to have been the law of the land before the Soviet colonisation of Central Asia; (2) it seemed only natural to institutionalise an important marker of Uzbek identity now that the Soviet implosion was facilitating expressions of national pride and sovereignty; and (3) the idea was appropriately unspecific, hence avoiding the risk of repulsing many Uzbeks who were uneasy about Islamic autocracy.

The Uzbek regime was wrong-footed by the audacity of the Islamic activists in the Ferghana Valley, who did not seem bound by the legalistic constraints affecting the IRP. For a few months in 1991 and 1992, the Uzbek leadership had little choice but to tolerate Yuldosh and his de facto rule over Namangan. But this uneasy state of affairs was untenable in the long run. President Islam Karimov must have been convinced of this after his encounter with Yuldosh and his supporters. While in Namangan in April 1991, Karimov agreed to address an Adolat rally. He was presented with a set of demands by Yuldosh:

> Islam Karimov must swear his faithfulness to Islam on the Koran and here and now proclaim an Islamic state, ... visiting mosques must become compulsory for all Muslims including leaders of the state who must pray together with the people, ... Friday should be announced as a day off, ... and open religious schools immediately.[7]

This experience must have shaken President Karimov and made him acutely aware of the potential challenge to his rule by Islamic activists. This concern with political legitimacy and a festering personal animosity between Karimov and Yuldosh/Namangani set the tone in the subsequent months. Adolat was banned in the first year of independence (March 1992) as the regime moved to eliminate its Islamic challengers and regain control over the Ferghana Valley.

The wave of repression that was initiated in 1992 forced many Islamic activists to escape the Ferghana Valley. Namangani chose to join the Islamic opposition movement in the Tajik civil war and proved himself to be an able field commander, capturing the strategically important Tavildara Valley on more than one occasion. In later years, following the cessation of hostilities in Tajikistan,

Namangani established a camp for his forces in Tavildara and used it for his campaign against President Karimov's regime. Yuldosh, on the other hand, travelled to Afghanistan, Pakistan and Saudi Arabia after his escape from the Ferghana Valley. According to Ahmed Rashid, Yuldosh was based in Peshawar between 1995 and 1998. In that period he enjoyed the support of Pakistani Islamists and met many Arabs who had joined the jihad against the Soviet invasion of Afghanistan.[8] It is believed that Yuldosh took advantage of his expanding networks to organise clandestine trips to the Ferghana Valley and the Surkhandarya district of Uzbekistan to maintain contact with his supporters and organise underground cells. The formation of the Islamic Movement of Uzbekistan (IMU) in 1998 brought together Namangani and Yuldosh, and their respective complementary networks and resources.

The IMU was staunchly anti-Karimov and defined its aim as the removal of *kafir* leaders from power in Tashkent and establishing an Islamic state.[9] The clandestine and guerrilla nature of IMU activities made it difficult for analysts to gain direct access to the organisation's members and literature. But a few key interviews and the publication of a two-page call to jihad have helped clarify IMU's mindset and objectives. In August 1999 a call to jihad was posted on the Internet by the IMU. It stated:

> The primary objective for this declaration of Jihad is the establishment of an Islamic state with the application of the Shariah, founded upon the Koran and the Noble Prophetic sunnah.[10]

The IMU declaration then called on 'the ruling government and Karimov leadership in Tashkent to remove itself from office – unconditionally, before the country enters into a state of war and destruction'. This document offers a rare insight into the mindset of the IMU leadership, as it avoids any mention of extending the campaign for Islamic rule to the rest of Central Asia. The jihad, as IMU portrays it, starts and ends in Uzbekistan. There has, of course, been an apparent inconsistency between this vision and the IMU's military operations in 1999–2001, as they were mostly conducted outside Uzbek territory. But the IMU declaration dismisses that contradiction as temporary and born out of tactical considerations, with no lasting impact on its Uzbekistan-centric views. It states:

The reason for the start of the Jihad in Kyrgyzstan ... [was] due to the stance of the ruler Askar Akayev Bishkek, in arresting thousands of Muslim Uzbeks who have migrated as refugees to Kyrgyzstan and were handed over to Karimov's henchmen.

The same view was expressed by Sherali Akbotoev, a leading member of the IMU, who was captured in May 2002 by the Kyrgyz security forces. In an interview with the London-based Institute of War and Peace in July 2002, Akbotoev said:

In my view, Namangani was mainly concerned with getting into Uzbekistan and the only way was through the Kyrgyz border. Attacking Kyrgyzstan was not part of the IMU leadership's overall plan, in my opinion. Battles could not be avoided, however, and without the heroism of Kyrgyz soldiers, the mojaheds would have reached Uzbekistan.[11]

Consequently, in the rare public statements made by the IMU leadership, the idea of a broad Central Asia-wide Islamic objective has been consistently rejected. This is a critical point, especially when the official media in the region reported that the IMU had upgraded its objectives to cover Central Asia and China's Muslim-populated Xinjiang, and changed its name to the Islamic Party of Turkestan. In a June 2001 interview with Radio Free Europe/Radio Liberty, Yuldosh's deputy, Zubair ibn Abdulrahim, conceded that 'there are many ethnic groups' in the ranks of the IMU. But he emphasised that his organisation has 'only one enemy – the Tashkent regime'. His response to charges of transnational agitation was categorical: 'we have no problems with neighbouring countries. Our name has not changed.'[12]

The IMU's focus on Uzbekistan was indicative of the extent to which Uzbek national consciousness was instrumental in giving shape to Islamic ideals. This national limitation is remarkable especially given Yoldush's extensive contacts with Islamists in South Asia and the Middle East. The limited scope of the Islamic ideal may also be partly due to the prevalent lack of ideological orientation of the IMU fighters and their motivations. According to Akbotoev, 'people rarely joined the IMU in the name of an ideal – it was a step they took mainly because of their poor living conditions'. He credits poverty and harsh living conditions in the Batken district of Kyrgyzstan as a major factor for the locals' receptiveness to the IMU. Ahmed

Rashid presents a similar picture when describing Namangani, not as a devout Muslim but as an action hero. Citing a close associate of Namangani, he observes:

> He [Juma Namangani] is essentially a guerrilla leader, not an Islamic scholar... He has been shaped by his own military and political experience rather than Islamic ideology but he hates the Uzbek government – that is what motivates him above all.[13]

Despite the air of mystery surrounding the IMU and its objectives, and fears of its potential to throw the whole region into chaos, it appears that its gaols and capacity to pursue them were much more limited than widely believed. The IMU was never able to present a serious challenge to President Karimov and his regime. In the wake of the American military operation in Afghanistan, the IMU's limited capacity has been seriously undermined. Juma Namangani was reported killed in the November 2001 bombing of Mazar-e Sharif and his forces are said to have been dispersed. There have been reports of the IMU regrouping in Tajikistan, but Russian journalists investigating these claims found no trace of illicit military activity in the suspected areas. Other reports claim that 3,000 IMU forces have blended into the local population of the Ferghana Valley, biding their time.[14] There could be some truth in the latter, although these reports are impossible to verify with any degree of certainty. At any rate the presence of the US armed forces in Central Asia, and substantially increased defence spending by Uzbekistan and Kyrgyzstan, thanks to US aid, means that the IMU would find it extremely difficult to launch new surprise operations. Much to the delight of President Karimov, the IMU threat has clearly declined.

The IMU was not the only Islamic party in Uzbekistan that pursued radical goals, and that was labelled Wahhabi by the regime. Since 1997–98 a new party has emerged on the scene with a truly revolutionary vision: Hizb al-Tahrir al-Islami (Islamic Liberation Party), commonly known as Hizb ut-Tahrir (HT). Hizb ut-Tahrir was originally linked to the Muslim Brotherhood. It was founded in 1952 by Taqi al-Din al-Nabahani in Jerusalem and was initially concerned with the cause of Palestinian liberation. But the logic of pursuing the boundless sovereignty of Allah led Hizb ut-Tahrir to go beyond existing state boundaries and champion the 'recreation of one Islamic state' to incorporate all Muslim societies.[15] The ideal of an Islamic caliphate harks back to the early history of Islam when all Muslims followed the prophet and his successors (caliphs). But the realisation of the caliphate throughout the Muslim world requires jihad against the prevalent corruption and kufr (disbelief) which have replaced the sharia and the Islamic way of life.[16] Hizb ut-Tahrir is aware that its universalist vision needs to be grounded in time and space in order for it to take shape and attain fulfilment:

> Although Islam is a universal ideology, its method does not … allow one to work for it universally from the beginning. It is necessary, however, to invite to it universally, and make the field of work for it in one country, or a few countries, until it is consolidated there and the Islamic State is established.[17]

This pragmatic approach has allowed Hizb ut-Tahrir to expand its presence in many Muslim societies, stretching from North Africa to Southeast Asia. The collapse of the Soviet Union and the opening of Central Asia to the outside world offered an opportunity for HT to infiltrate this region. The secretive nature of HT in Central Asia makes it difficult to ascertain how it spearheaded its entry into this region. It is quite likely that HT relied on exiled Central Asians (primarily Uzbek) in Pakistan, Turkey and Saudi Arabia to form a vanguard and deliver its message back home. Whatever its entry tactic, HT's message of social justice and Islamic unity appears to have found resonance among Uzbek youth who are being alienated by the absence of employment prospects and the failure of the social security system to protect them against the adverse effects of the market economy. Consequently, the projected Islamic state in Uzbekistan, a step towards creating an ideal transnational caliphate, appeals to devout Muslims who feel betrayed by the government of President Karimov.

HT rejects violence as a means of achieving its objectives. This strategy has proved to be its greatest asset in Central Asia, as well as in the broader context. Its nonviolent campaign and seemingly moderate approach to politics – which does not espouse religious wars, ethnic favouritism, discrimination against women and favours democratic practices – have made HT an attractive choice. HT membership in Uzbekistan is believed to be on the rise, especially in the wake of the American involvement in the region. The party puts the figure at over 100,000 members in Uzbekistan,[18] including 10,000 in Uzbek jails.[19] These figures are impossible to verify, and the HT leadership itself would have difficulty in arriving at an exact number because members are divided into groups of autonomous cells, each comprising three to five members, with little horizontal contact; cell leaders link up with a higher tier in a pyramidal structure.

Needless to say, HT's nonviolent strategy did not enable it to become a legal organisation in Uzbekistan and its neighbouring republics, but it has allowed the party to operate openly with the full protection of the law in Europe, primarily in Britain where its head office is based. This freedom has allowed HT to conduct a propaganda campaign against the Uzbek regime, aimed at influencing Western public opinion and human rights organisations. Examples of HT's Uzbekistan-related activities include a poster campaign to highlight the torture and murder of a HT activist in Tashkent (June 1999), 'Who Killed Farhad Usmanov?', and a public seminar in London (July 2002) to expose President Karimov's 'cruel campaign against all those who dare to oppose his despotic rule'. It is clear that HT's transnational character is a significant contributory factor to its ability to operate in the inhospitable political environment of Uzbekistan. The discovery of an underground printing press in Tajikistan's northern province of Soghd in January 2003, equipped with high-tech desktop publishing facilities and a large quantity of Uzbek-language pamphlets and leaflets, demonstrated further the ease with which HT could operate transnationally.[20]

The Uzbek regime has insisted for many years that HT is an extremist organisation with links to the IMU.[21] Tashkent has lobbied Russia, the European Community and the United States to list HT as terrorist. Unlike the clear case of the IMU, that presented against HT is unconvincing and Western powers have been reluctant to comply with Tashkent's requests. Some media reports from the region, however, seem to support Tashkent's claims. *Pravda* reported, for example, that arrests and investigations by Kyrgyz security forces have found incriminating evidence to link extremism in the Osh and Jelal-Abad provinces with HT in Uzbekistan.[22] This link was confirmed by Uzbek refugees, now in Kyrgyzstan. According to Radio Free Europe/Radio Liberty, the Tajik security services have also claimed such links following the discovery of pertinent evidence in that republic.[23] Although it is difficult to verify these claims, they may contain some truth, given the radically changed political environment in the region following the arrival of American troops in 2001.

Bakhtiyar Bobojonov of the Tashkent Academy of Sciences argues that the US-led anti-terrorism campaign which began in Afghanistan and brought US forces to Uzbekistan made a profound impact on Hizb ut-Tahrir: 'After the campaign against terrorists started in Afghanistan, the position of Hizb ut-Tahrir changed and they became much more radical. They are spreading leaflets and literature calling for war and martyrdom in the war for Islam.'[24] As HT members and sympathisers find themselves increasingly under pressure from the regime, now bolstered by US support, it is not implausible that they will become increasingly alienated from the international community and tend to 'sympathise with the IMU and its military struggle in particular'.[25]

The radicalisation of HT's tactics suggests a dangerous trend, set in motion as a consequence of the policies of the ruling elite in Uzbekistan. Tashkent's repressive measures against autonomous Islamic activity and the current ties between Uzbekistan and the United States, seen by many Uzbeks as the international community's endorsement of President Karimov's leadership, have transformed the quasi-Islamic movement of the early 1990s into a more ideologically inspired force in the early 2000s. Within a decade Islamism in Uzbekistan has grown to be a real force with broad implications for that state and the region as a whole. It is ironic that Tashkent's policies of repression and intolerance have, by default, nurtured what it feared the most.

Notes

1. Interview with Abdullah Utaev, leader of the IRP in Uzbekistan, Tashkent, 10 October 1992.
2. Olivier Roy, *The Foreign Policy of Central Asian Islamic Renaissance Party* (New York: Council on Foreign Relations, 2000), p. 13.
3. In a series of media interviews in 1990 and 1991, the Mufti of Central Asia, Muhammad Yusuf, rejected the idea that Islam could serve as a platform for political activity. This was the official view under Soviet rule and was endorsed by the post-Soviet regime of President Karimov. He told the Soviet newspaper *Komsomol'skaya Pravda* that Muslims already had a party: Islam. 'It would be wrong to form a party under the pretext of Islam because that would inevitably lead to divisions among Muslims.

Islam transcends earthly categories of clubs and parties.' He never recanted that view even after the Soviet collapse. 'My-partiya Allakha', *Komsomol'skaya Pravda*, 8 December 1990, p. 1.

4. 'Ob obshchestvennykh ob''edineniyakh v Uzbekskoi SSR', *Pravda Vostoka*, 26 February 1991, p. 2.

5. This point is explored extensively in Shahram Akbarzade, 'Islamic Clerical Establishment in Central Asia', *South Asia*, vol. 20, no. 2, December 1997, pp. 73–102.

6. Viktoria Panfilova, 'Grazhdane yaponii obreli svobodu', *Nezavisimaya Gazeta*, 26 October 1999.

7. Quoted in Ahmed Rashid, *Jihad: The Rise of Militant Islam in Central Asia* (New Haven, CT: Yale University Press, 2002), pp. 255–6.

8. Ibid., p. 140.

9. International Crisis Group (ICG), *The IMU and the Hizb-ut Tahrir: Implications of the Afghanistan Campaign*, Central Asia Briefing, Osh/Brussels, 30 January 2002.

10. The document, 'The Call to Jihad by the Islamic Movement of Uzbekistan', is reproduced in Rashid, *Jihad*, pp. 247–9; see Appendix C below.

11. Institute for War and Peace Reporting, 'IMU Insight', *Reporting Central Asia*, 12 July 2002.

12. Bruce Pannier, 'Central Asia: IMU Leader Says Group's Goal is "Return of Islam"', Radio Free Europe/Radio Liberty, 6 June 2001.

13. Rashid, *Jihad*, p. 143.

14. Armen Khanbaian and Mikhail Khodarenok, 'Pered geostrategicheskoi razvilkoi. Tashkent vinuzhden lavirovat' mezhdu Rossiei i zapodom', *Nezavisimaya Gazeta*, 15 April 2002.

15. See Dale F. Eickelman and James Piscatori, *Muslim Politics* (Princeton, NJ: Princeton University Press, 1996), p. 139.

16. Hizb ut-Tahrir's web page offers this categorical explanation: 'Muslims nowadays live in Dar al-Kufr, because they are governed with laws other than the revelation of Allah (swt)', www.hizb-ut-tahrir.org.

17. See Hizb ut-Tahrir webpage, www.hizb-ut-tahrir.org.

18. Alexei Igushev, 'Hizb-ut-Tahrir Remains Active in Central Asia', EurasiaNet. Org, 4 February 2003, www.eurasianet.org.

19. 'Karimov plans to exterminate Hizb ut-Tahrir by November', 14 August 2002, www.muslimuzbekistan.com.

20. 'Clandestine Print Shop Raided in Tajikistan', Radio Free Europe/Radio Liberty, 3 February 2003.

21. Bruce Pannier, 'How Big a Threat is Hizb ut-Tahrir?' Radio Free Europe/Radio Liberty, 30 May 2002.

22. Yury Razgulyaev, 'V kirgizii aktivizirovalis' radikal'nye Islamisty', *Pravda*, 11 June 2002.

23. Charles Carlson, 'Kyrgyzstan: Hizb ut-Tahrir Accused of Increased Militancy', Radio Free Europe/Radio Liberty, 3 March 2003.

24. Bruce Pannier, 'Central Asia: Governments React to Uncertain Threat from Hizb ut-Tahrir', Radio Free Europe/Radio Liberty, 30 May 2002.

25. Ibragim Alibekov, 'IMU Reportedly Expands, Prepares to Strike Western Targets', EurasiaNet.Org, 29 October 2002, www.eurasianet.org.

3

Tashkent's Foreign Policy Decisions

Tashkent's foreign policy was heavily influenced by its preoccupation with Islam. The civil war in Tajikistan had a formative impact on the Uzbek leadership. It highlighted the threat that political Islam appeared to pose to the ruling regime and its continued hold on society. The Tajik experience, followed by the fall of Kabul to the Taliban, convinced Tashkent that countering the Islamic threat would have to be central to its foreign-policy agenda. Uzbekistan's behaviour in relation to Tajikistan and subsequent foreign-relations initiatives in Afghanistan were heavily influenced by the fear of being overwhelmed by Islamic contenders to power. Many observers questioned the real extent of the so-called Islamic menace, and Tashkent's Western interlocutors, by and large, remained sceptical about Uzbekistan's hidden agenda in highlighting the threat of Islamic extremism as a pretext for the absence of political openness. In fact President Karimov made a direct link between his country's slow pace of democratic reform and the dangers of Islamic extremism emanating from its neighbours. In April 2000, addressing his Central Asian counterparts, Karimov argued:

> while war is in progress there [in Afghanistan], while the most dangerous fanatics and bandits are concentrating there, how can we seriously engage in matters of renovation and democratic transformation and how can we calmly create a market economy and integrate into the world economy?[1]

In the first decade of independence, the Uzbek leadership lobbied the United Nations and Western leaders to take the danger of Islamic extremism in Central Asia seriously. But its success was limited. The September 11 attacks on the United States by al-Qaeda and the retaliatory US operation in Afghanistan against Osama bin Laden and his Taliban backers led to a marked change in the international political landscape in favour of Tashkent's foreign policy. President Karimov drew satisfaction from the belated international response to terrorism, which his leadership interpreted as a realisation of the perils of political Islam and approval of his policies.

Responding to the Tajik Civil War

Tashkent took an openly confrontational stance in relation to the Islamic/democratic opposition movement in Tajikistan. It refused to recognise the short-lived National Reconciliation Government which gave opposition leaders a share in power between May and November 1992. Instead Tashkent offered military hardware and support to anti-Islamic/democratic forces in their campaign against the Reconciliation Government. In October 1992 Safarali Kenjaev, the deposed chair of Tajikistan's Supreme Soviet, launched an unsuccessful attack on Dushanbe from Uzbek territory. In the subsequent months Uzbek fighter jets bombed opposition strongholds in Kafirnihon and Gharm.[2] Incursions into Tajik airspace were justified by Tashkent's formal adoption of responsibility for providing air security for Tajikistan due to 'exceptional circumstances'.[3] Reports indicate that by February 1993 Tashkent also sent reinforcements to assist Dushanbe in sealing the Tajik–Afghan border after the opposition forces fled across the Amu Darya river to Afghanistan.[4] Tashkent's response to developments in Tajikistan was prompt and effective. It moved to consolidate its air-security responsibilities in Tajikistan in March 1993,[5] and to draw international support for its involvement in the Tajik civil war.

Tashkent urged Russia to take a more active role in repulsing the 'fundamentalist threat'. In an interview with the Russian press, Islam Karimov rhetorically asked whether it might be possible that the Russian government was betraying Russians in Tajikistan and allowing Central Asia to slide into the anarchy of fundamentalism.[6] Tashkent's lobby added weight to pro-interventionist voices in Moscow and led to a concerted effort to repel the Islamic threat in Tajikistan. Against this background, the formation of a Collective Peacekeeping Force was announced at a CIS summit in November 1993.[7] The peacekeeping force was expected to consist of troops from Kyrgyzstan, Kazakhstan, Russia and Uzbekistan. But, in effect, it was overwhelmingly drawn from Russian troops, including the 201 Russian Division, already stationed in Tajikistan. Uzbekistan's contribution to this force during its mandate (1993–98) remained minimal: one company, according to Russian sources.[8] The first battalion of CIS peacekeeping forces arrived in Tajikistan on 3 March 1993 and stationed itself in the mountain-ous Gorno-Badakhshan, the scene of cross-border incursions from Afghanistan by Tajik opposition units.[9]

Uzbekistan was very keen to gain UN approval for the peacekeep-ing operation in Tajikistan. But despite repeated requests for UN backing of these operations, the United Nations refused to grant the peacekeepers its formal blessing,[10] perhaps being mindful of the close association between the peacekeeping force and the government of Emomali Rahmonov in Dushanbe. The United Nations, however, endorsed efforts to bring the civil war to a close. Interestingly, Tashkent's approach to these efforts appeared ambivalent. Uzbekistan was an observer in the UN-sponsored peace talks to end the Tajik civil war. But during this period (1994–97) Uzbekistan showed little enthusiasm for the talks to succeed. It frequently absented itself from meetings and in 1997 it delayed the signing of a protocol that named Uzbekistan, along with ten other states and international organisations, the guarantor of peace in Tajikistan.[11] Some observ-ers argue that this reluctance was due to Tashkent's dissatisfaction with the exclusion from the peace process of regional leaders from Leninabad, who have traditionally been close to Tashkent.[12] While this was a concern for Uzbek foreign-policymakers, prospects of a political settlement allowing the incorporation of Islamic forces in the government of Tajikistan, according to the terms of the peace treaty, must have been extremely threatening to the Uzbek leadership in Tashkent. The June 1997 agreement to end the civil war stipulated a transitional quota system that reserved 30 per cent of all local, regional and central government posts for the opposition movement, primarily staffed by Islamists. It also called for the lifting of the ban on Islamic partisanship and reform of the Constitution to remove restrictions on religious political mobilisation.[13] These measures were unique in Central Asia, and Karimov and his cohorts were no doubt concerned about the precedent that they were setting. Later events – for example, the formation of the IMU and its operation from Tajik territory – seemed to substantiate Tashkent's fears regarding the destabilising impact of placing Islamists in positions of authority in Tajikistan. Tashkent especially targeted Mizo Ziyoev, Tajik minister of emergency situations and a former field commander with the Tajik opposition, for his ties to Namangani and accused him of providing protection to IMU forces, a charge that was vehemently denied by Ziyoev and the Tajik government.[14]

Afghanistan

The other external Islamic challenge that occupied Tashkent was posed from Afghanistan. The fall of Kabul to the Taliban in September 1996 brought to power a staunchly puritan movement with ambiguous intentions toward its neighbours to the north. The imposition of strict sharia law in the Taliban-controlled territory and the summary public execution of Muhammad Najibullah sent shock waves through the Central Asian capitals.[15] The Uzbek leadership was particularly alarmed by the Taliban's northward advance towards ethnic Uzbek forces under General Abdul Rashid Dostum.[16] In a hastily organised summit between Russia and four Central Asian republics in Almaty (Kazakhstan) only a week after the fall of Kabul, President Karimov urged on his counterparts coordinated action and support for General Dostum's forces. In his view, Dostum offered the best fighting force to stop the Taliban advance and the best chance of separating that extremist movement from the borders of the Central Asian republics.[17] In other words, Dostum's defence of the Salang Pass in central Afghanistan was in effect protecting the CIS countries.[18]

At the same time Tashkent was mindful of the opportunities this new development was creating for Russia to consolidate, even expand, its military presence in Central Asia under the pretext of protecting the region against Islamic extremism. In response to Russian media speculations that the Taliban were poised to invade Uzbekistan and occupy the area around Buhkara, President Karimov retorted:

I do not take seriously the claim that the Taliban want to conquer a part of Uzbek territory.... It is hard to believe that such assessment could have been made in the first place. Uzbekistan has its own armed forces and with the assistance of its friends can rebuff any aggression.[19]

President Karimov repeated his scepticism regarding Moscow's hidden agenda in the way it portrayed the danger from the south. In a statement issued in October 2000, Karimov called on Russian leaders to stop intimidating Uzbekistan and other Central Asian republics with speculation about the Taliban. He claimed the danger was being grossly exaggerated by Moscow for its own geostrategic objectives.[20] But at the same time his leadership could not afford to be complacent about the Taliban.

Tashkent moved quickly to strengthen the controls on its border with Afghanistan. By early 1997 the Uzbek regime had achieved a high degree of readiness with a mass mobilisation.[21] Conditions appeared to take a turn for the worse in May 1997 when the Taliban entered General Dostum's key city of Mazar-e Sharif, forcing him to take refuge in Turkey.[22] The Taliban were now in control of the territories adjacent to Uzbekistan. Although the Taliban's hold on Mazar-e Sharif proved tenuous and they were forced to retreat only a week after entering General Dostum's stronghold, they managed to capture the city again in August 1998. It seemed to international observers and Central Asian leaders that the Uzbek and Tajik forces resisting the Taliban advance were fighting a losing battle.

Tashkent's response to these ominous developments was first and foremost to reinforce its border protection. Uzbek leaders also turned to the international arena to gain support for their position and involve the international community in curtailing the regional impact of the Taliban ascendancy in Afghanistan and ultimately diluting the Taliban's power by implementing a policy of national reconciliation aimed at establishing a multi-ethnic regime. Uzbekistan's international campaign against Afghanistan was double-pronged. First, it identified Pakistan as the main pillar of support for the Taliban and tried to shame it into a policy reversal. Second, it lobbied the United States and other Western powers, as well as the UN, to take action in Afghanistan in order to address the growing links between the Taliban and 'international terrorist' organisations and the production and trafficking of narcotics.

At the May 1997 Central Asian Summit, for example, President Karimov lashed out at Pakistan for supporting the Taliban and denounced 'external meddling' in Afghanistan. Addressing Pakistan's prime minister, Nawaz Sharif, also present at the summit, Karimov demanded he order his government to stop supporting the Taliban.[23] This became a recurring charge by the Uzbek government in its relations with Pakistan in subsequent years.

The Uzbek leadership was very sensitive to reports that the IMU had found a safe haven in the Taliban-controlled territories. These reports made Tashkent even more determined to offset the growing threat posed by the Taliban. The Uzbek leadership must have been aware that the charge of harbouring terrorists levelled against the Taliban had the potential to resonate in Western capitals and win support; Tashkent made every effort to take advantage of this leverage. In July 1999 President Karimov stated that 'the world community is worried about what is going on in and around Afghanistan, notably the rise in international terrorism and extremism, drugs and arms trafficking and the radicalization of Islam.'[24] Karimov was keenly aware of the mood in the US administration. In August 1998 President Bill Clinton had ordered an attack on al-Qaeda training camps in Afghanistan in retaliation for the bombing of US embassies in Tanzania and Kenya. Terrorism was becoming an important international concern for the United States and the rest of the world, and Tashkent opted to frame its opposition to the Taliban regime in such rhetoric that was familiar to the United States. In June 2000 President Karimov used the occasion of a Central Asian summit in Tajikistan to reiterate the charge that Afghanistan had become a safe haven and a training ground for international terrorists who could operate globally.[25]

Tashkent had adopted the view, immediately after the fall of Kabul, that the Taliban regime was illegitimate and the resolution of the Afghan predicament depended on the formation of a government of national reconciliation with the participation of all ethnic, religious and regional groups.[26] This principle was obviously intended to facilitate the political representation of Afghanistan's Uzbek minority – that is, Tashkent's natural allies. But the principle was formulated in a language that conformed to international norms of political freedom and participation, and Tashkent skilfully used this platform to launch an international campaign against Afghanistan. In 1998, after intense lobbying by Tashkent, the United Nations agreed to sponsor the formation of the Six plus Two group, which included six regional states neighbouring Afghanistan (China, Iran, Pakistan, Tajikistan, Turkmenistan and Uzbekistan) and the two great powers with interests in Afghanistan (Russia and the United States). In July 1999 the Six plus Two group met in Tashkent and endorsed, in effect, Uzbekistan's position on the establishment of a 'multi-ethnic and fully representative government on a wide basis'; protection of human rights in accordance with international law; and expulsion of terrorists from Afghanistan.[27] This joint document, known as the Tashkent Declaration, added further weight to Uzbekistan's international campaign against Afghanistan.

Yet in 2000, with no prospects of change in sight, Tashkent appeared to re-evaluate its policy on Afghanistan. In an apparent about-face, it announced its readiness to establish diplomatic relations with the Taliban regime. The Russian news agency Itar-Tass quoted President Karimov:

> Tashkent is prepared to recognise any Afghan government, be it even a Taliban one. It does not matter whether we like that government or not…. To judge which government suits the people of that long-suffering country is the Afghan people's internal affair, in which Uzbekistan does not intend to intervene.[28]

However, this conciliatory tone made no significant impact on relations between the Uzbek leadership and the Taliban. President Karimov continued to view the Taliban with suspicion, especially given the latter's support for Namangani and the IMU. For that reason, the Uzbek leadership did not hesitate the following year to lend its support to the United States in the 'war on terror', which resulted in the toppling of the Taliban and the reported death of Namangani.

Seeking International Support

Tashkent's Islamophobia was a determining factor in the way it conducted its international relations. Home-grown Islamic opposition activists, the civil war in Tajikistan and the military gains of the Taliban in Afghanistan convinced Tashkent of the need to seek friends and partners who shared its views on the dangers of Islamic radicalism to the region. This assessment corresponded with the Russian approach to the Islamic challenge. Despite their differences, Moscow and Tashkent found common cause in the Tajik civil war. They supported Emomali Rahmonov against the coalition of Islamic and democratic forces and ensured his victory. But this convergence of interests did not stand the test of time as Tashkent grew increasingly concerned about (1) Russia's entrenchment in the region, and (2) Russia's inability to initiate a serious counterinsurgency plan against the Islamists. These considerations explain in part Tashkent's search for allies further afield – for instance, Uzbekistan's entry into the Shanghai Cooperation Organisation (June 2001) and the signing of a formal security treaty with the United States (March 2002).

Russia/CIS

To say that Uzbekistan had a difficult relationship with Russia would be an understatement.[29] The Uzbek leadership recognised that Moscow feared the growth of Islamic insurgency in Central Asia as much as Tashkent, and this made Russia a natural ally. In an interview with the Russian daily *Nezavisimaya Gazeta*, President Karimov acknowledged that Russia was the main guarantor of peace and stability in Central Asia.[30] Moscow's determination to prevent the establishment of an Islamic state in its southern tier coincided with Tashkent's strategy of repelling Islamists from Tajik territory. This coincidence of interests benefited Rahmonov's forces, which captured Dushanbe in December 1992 and relied on Russian and CIS peacekeeping forces for protection in subsequent years.

The deteriorating civil unrest in Tajikistan in the early part of 1992, before the onset of the civil war, provided the background to the formation of the CIS Collective Security Treaty (CST). At the time, Tashkent felt it necessary to join the only power available in order to protect itself. Its participation in the CIS CST, which was formally launched in May 1992, reflected the prevalent view among Uzbek leaders that the Islamic threat was too great to be faced alone. But Tashkent's relationship with Russia, the senior partner in the CIS CST, was fraught with tension. While the Uzbek leadership did not wish to face the Islamic threat alone, Russia's military presence in Tajikistan was seen as creating obstacles to Uzbekistan's regional ambitions. Two important episodes magnified the divergence of interests in the Uzbek–Russian anti-Islamic coalition.

The first was the gradual marginalisation of the leaders from Leninabad who had traditionally been close to Tashkent, with Russia's tacit approval. Emomali Rahmonov's first government after capturing Dushanbe included Abdumalik Abdullojonov, a well-known Leninabadi politician, in the post of prime minister. But a mere twelve months later he was dismissed on charges of financial misconduct and corruption.[31] Abdullojonov subsequently lost the 1994 presidential elections, dismissed by international observers as rigged, and was later barred from contending the parliamentary elections on the grounds of the judicial proceedings against him. His elimination from Tajikistan's political life revealed Rahmonov's determination to prevent the return of Leninabadis to positions of leadership. Rahmonov's agenda became even more evident in his refusal to accept a tripartite basis for the peace talks. Much to the dissatisfaction of Tashkent, the eventual peace treaty completely bypassed Leninabad. The Uzbek leadership had lost its allies in Dushanbe and was unable to make a meaningful impression on the Tajik leadership. Instead the latter was increasingly relying on Russia and its troops in Tajikistan to protect itself physically (from Islamic forces) and politically (from Tashkent).

It soon became clear to the Uzbek leadership that Russia's involvement in Tajikistan had far greater implications than countering the Islamic threat. This was the second critical factor in Tashkent's foreign policy planning. Russia's presence in Tajikistan was allowing Dushanbe to resist pressure from Tashkent, and to break the pattern of acquiescence that signified relations between the two Central Asian neighbours. Tashkent feared that Moscow was using the Tajik civil war as a pretext for its continued military presence in the region. This fear may have been behind the May 1995 announcement that Uzbek and Kazakh troops would withdraw from the CIS peacekeeping mission if the Tajik government failed to make progress in peace talks.[32] In effect, Uzbekistan could not extract itself from Tajik affairs as that would have left Tajikistan even more open to Russian influence. Only after the signing of the peace treaty and the

Figure 3.1 Timeline of Uzbekistan's membership of strategic and security organisations

May 1992	Enters CIS CST
April 1999	Leaves CIS CST
April 1999	Enters GUUAM
June 2001	Enters SOC
March 2002	US–Uzbek Strategic Partnership
June 2002	Intention to leave GUUAM, but is dissuaded

secession of hostilities did Tashkent withdraw its small battalion that was serving with the CIS peacekeeping force in Tajikistan.[33] Tashkent expected Russia to follow suit and was particularly incensed when it learned of a bilateral security arrangement that granted Russia permission to maintain a military base in Tajikistan for twenty-five years.[34] The Russo–Tajik treaty entrenched Russia in the region – an unambiguous affront to Tashkent's long-term objective of replacing Moscow as the regional hegemon.

Tashkent's regional ambitions were clearly being thwarted by Moscow's refusal to withdraw from Central Asia. The Uzbek leadership had already asserted its independence by taking responsibility for the protection for its 350-kilometre frontier with Afghanistan. But it appeared unprepared to respond to major challenges beyond Uzbek frontiers. The growing tension between Tashkent and Moscow over Tajikistan provided the background to Tashkent's announcement of its intention to withdraw from the CIS CST in February 1999.[35] Tashkent claimed that the CIS CST had become a tool for Russian hegemony.[36] Uzbekistan's refusal to renew its membership of the CIS CST at the April CIS summit was the culmination of a long process, during which the Uzbek leadership continually reassessed the tangible benefits and costs of maintaining security ties with Russia against the perceived Islamic threat.

International organisations

In 1999 Uzbekistan was still looking for allies to combat Islamic insurgency as well as counter Russia's entrenchment in Central Asia.

In April 1999, soon after leaving the CIS CST, it joined Georgia, Ukraine, Azerbaijan and Moldova in GUUAM.[37] The participating states adopted an ambitious charter in June 2001 which provided for trade and economic integration, regional security, combating terrorism and organised crime and a host of other objectives.[38] But GUUAM was effectively a talking shop with no permanent secretariat and no tangible structure to push through collective decisions. The real significance of GUUAM was symbolic. All member states had past or current disputes with Russia, and Uzbekistan's decision to join this anti-Russian group made explicit its antipathy towards Moscow. However, symbolism alone proved to be insufficient grounds for Tashkent's continued commitment to GUUAM, and in June 2002 Tashkent announced its decision to leave the organisation.[39] This announcement came against the background of the war in Afghanistan and the de facto alliance between Uzbekistan and the United States. It is interesting to note that Tashkent's decision was subsequently reversed after suggestions by the United States that GUUAM had a future and that it would be beneficial for Uzbekistan to remain part of it – hinting at Washington's long-term plans to prop up this coalition of anti-Russian states.[40]

The growing intensity of Islamic insurgency in late 1999 and 2000 gave Tashkent's response to the question of 'Islamic threat' pressing urgency. Suspicious of Moscow's hidden agenda in Central Asia and its dominating role in the CIS CST, and disillusioned with the prospects of meaningful assistance from their GUUAM partners, Uzbek leaders felt compelled to look for other allies. The newly formed Shanghai Five, with China in the leading role, appeared an attractive option. The Shanghai Five was a regional confidence-building organisation, formed in 1996 by Russia, China, Kazakhstan, Kyrgyzstan and Tajikistan. It was originally aimed at dismantling military build-up and defusing tension on the former Sino–Soviet border, now inherited by successor Soviet states. But trans-border incursions into Kyrgyzstan's Batken district in 1999 and the intensification of Islamic guerrilla activity in 2000 led that organisation to take a strong 'anti-terrorist' position – quite similar to that of Uzbekistan. This convergence of interests against a common enemy made possible Uzbekistan's admission (as an observer state) to the Shanghai Five in 2000, even though Uzbekistan did not share a border with China. Following

Uzbekistan's formal entry in June 2001, that organisation changed its name to the Shanghai Cooperation Organisation (SCO), also known as the Shanghai Forum.[41]

Three distinct but interrelated considerations appear to have contributed to Tashkent's decision to join the Shanghai group: Tashkent's desire to limit Moscow's ability to influence the region, its pressing fear of a growing Islamic insurgency, and regional prestige. The first two were not readily compatible. Moscow's ability to exercise undue pressure on Uzbekistan within the framework of the SCO was deemed to have been curtailed by the presence of Beijing as a counterforce in the organisation. But as years passed and summit after summit passed resolutions against the threat of Islamic terrorism and separatism, this concern seemed to remain practically unattended. Although the Uzbek leadership did not feel vulnerable to pressure from Moscow within the SCO, it gained no tangible benefits in combating Islamic insurgency. The SCO failed to make any impact on the IMU forces operating in the region. A revealing demonstration of the SCO's lack of agility to deal with the Islamic threat was its sluggish pace in establishing an anti-terrorist centre. The long awaited anti-terrorist centre only received its official backing at the June 2002 summit when the organisation finally approved that initiative and designated Bishkek to host it.[42] This decision came following the successful American campaign in Afghanistan and the establishment of American military presence in Kyrgyzstan, Tajikistan and Uzbekistan.[43] It is revealing to note that just over a year later the SCO voted to move the planned anti-terrorist centre to Tashkent. No reason was given for this decision, but it is likely to have been designed to tie Uzbekistan closely to Russia and China, as a countermeasure to Tashkent's partnership with the United States.[44]

The third factor influencing Tashkent's decision to join the SCO was prestige, in line with Uzbekistan's self-perception as the regional leader. As such, it was inconceivable for Uzbekistan not to be part of this regional organisation which, in its early days, promised to become an influential international player. From President Karimov's point of view, Uzbekistan was integral to any viable regional initiative. He put it thus:

> Currently 50 million people live in the Central Asian region. If we consider that half of those people live in Uzbekistan and that Uzbekistan has a

key geopolitical location in the region, sharing borders with almost all members of the 'Shanghai Five', and if we consider the interests of the 'Shanghai Five' member states – it is first and foremost in their interest that Uzbekistan join this organisation.[45]

However, Tashkent appears to be distancing itself from the SCO because it essentially failed in its anti-Islamism agenda. Tashkent also feels that the existing regional framework is not sufficient to keep Russian hegemonic tendencies in check, as discussed in Chapter 5. Uzbekistan's decision not to partake in the SCO anti-terrorist military exercises, held in August 2003, may have been a sign of this frustration.[46]

Conclusion

Uzbek foreign policy was slow to take shape and adopt a clear direction. Two key factors seemed to drive that policy, sometimes in opposite directions. The Uzbek leadership was deeply concerned with developments in Tajikistan and Afghanistan, and their implications for the spread of Islamic insurgency throughout the region, especially to Uzbekistan. Erecting diplomatic as well as military barriers against political Islam became a cornerstone of Tashkent's foreign policy.[47] The other competing concern centred around the Uzbek leadership's perception of Uzbekistan as a regional power and the commensurate regional ambitions which came into conflict with Russia's continued influence in Central Asia. Tashkent's pursuit of its twin objectives was a difficult juggling act. As a general rule, the second objective was often overshadowed by the perceived urgency of the Islamic threat. Uzbek policymakers found themselves, against their better judgement, approaching Moscow for assistance in dealing with the Islamic threat in Tajikistan and Afghanistan. Despite Tashkent's efforts to forge counterbalancing partnerships against Russia, it was blatantly clear to Uzbek leaders that they could not make a clear break with Moscow. This was far from satisfactory for Tashkent, because relying on Russia to ensure security (1) had the potential to entangle Tashkent in Russian-dominated organisations, and (2) proved ultimately ineffective in achieving Tashkent's primary objective of eradicating the Islamic threat.

Tashkent was of course aware of the limitations of, and the risks involved in, its association with Russia. The Uzbek leadership felt that alliance with Russia, uncomfortable and turbulent as it must have been, was the best it could achieve. Henry Hale has argued that geography and the existing economic infrastructure destined Uzbekistan to remain close to Russia in its early years of independence. Tashkent's foreign policy, Hale argued in 1994, was 'likely [to] remain primarily oriented towards Russia'.[48] But far from a long-term strategic alignment, security ties with Russia were a stop-gap measure. Even in the early stages, Tashkent's discomfort with Russia was salient. Instead of Russia, Tashkent oriented its foreign policy towards the United States and, as will be discussed in Chapter 4, made initial overtures to join the NATO bloc in 1994.[49] As far as Tashkent was concerned the United States was the ideal partner. The United States shared Uzbekistan's assessment of the dangers of Islamic extremism and could help Tashkent pursue its dual agenda of fighting Islamism and expanding its regional reach. But this partnership remained illusive. The major impediment to close bilateral relations was the US perception of Uzbekistan as a country of little geostrategic significance ruled by an authoritarian regime. It was this assessment that made Tashkent's chances of finding a counterbalance to Russia bleak. As Gail W. Lapidus has argued, in the pre-September 11 environment, 'however well-disposed any given US administration might … [have been], the United States was ultimately a distant and uncertain partner, whereas Russia, by geography, by history and by political, economic, and security interests, was likely to continue to play a considerable role in the region.'[50] The following chapter will explore issues that informed US policy towards Uzbekistan.

Notes

1. http://uzland.narod.ru/2000/04_22.htm.
2. Bess Brown, 'Tajik Opposition to Be Banned', *RFE/RL Research Report*, vol. 2, no. 14, 2 April 1993, p. 11
3. Interfax News Agency, 23 December 1992.
4. Radio Free Europe/Radio Liberty, 1 March 1993.
5. Itar-Tass News Agency, 25 March 1993.
6. 'Suverennost', kotoraya ob'edinyaet', *Vek*, 22 October 1992, p. 3.
7. Alexander Sokolov, 'Russian Peace-Keeping Forces in the Post-Soviet

Area', in Mary Kaldor and Basker Vashee, eds, *Restructuring the Global Military Sector*, Vol. I (London and Washington DC: New Wars Printer, 1997).

8. *Nezavisimoe Voennoe Obozrenie*, 16 July 1998. It is not immediately clear why Uzbekistan took such a low profile in the CIS Peacekeeping Force once it was created. This might be related to Tashkent's uneasiness about placing Uzbek forces under Russian command while it was trying to establish control over its own border with Afghanistan and asking Moscow to withdraw its border guards from Uzbek territory.

9. Radio Free Europe/Radio Liberty, 4 March 1993.

10. Lena Jonson, 'Russian Policy and Tajikistan', *Central Asia*, vol. 8, no. 2, 1997; www.ca-c.org/dataeng/st_03_jonson.shtml.

11. Radio Free Europe/Radio Liberty, 25 July 1997. Other guarantors (known as the Contact Group) included Afghanistan, Iran, Kazakhstan, Kyrgyz Republic, Pakistan, Russia, Turkmenistan, the United Nations, the Organisation of Islamic Conference, and the Organisation of Security and Cooperation in Europe.

12. Stuart Horsman, 'Uzbekistan's Involvement in the Tajik Civil war 1992–97: Domestic Considerations', *Central Asian Survey*, vol. 18, no. 1, 1999, p. 41.

13. Kamoludin Abdullaev and Shahram Akbarzadeh, *Historical Dictionary of Tajikistan* (Lanham, MD: Scarecrow Press, 2002), pp. 71, 93.

14. Bruce Pannier and Salimjon Aioubov, 'Tajikistan: Opposition Leader Responds to Charges from Uzbekistan', RFE/RL, *Newsline*, 4 June 1999.

15. Najibullah was president of Afghanistan between 1987 and 1992. After Russia stopped aid to Najibullah, his government collapsed under the weight of sustained mujahidin attacks on Kabul (1992). Najibullah took refuge in the UN compound for over four years. In September 1996 he and his bodyguard were dragged out of the UN compound by the Taliban and hanged from a lamppost.

16. *Sovetskaya Rossia*, 1 October 1996, p. 3.

17. *Segodnya*, 8 October 1996, p. 2.

18. *Komsomol'skaya Pravda*, 6 October 1996, p. 1.

19. *Kommersant-Daily*, 13 November 1996, p. 26.

20. *Rossiiskaya Gazeta*, 10 October 2000, pp. 1, 7.

21. Agence France Presse, 28 February 1997.

22. *Courier-Mail*, 27 May 1997, p. 18.

23. Agence France Presse, 14 May 1997.

24. Interfax News Agency, 19 July 1999.

25. The Central Asian Economic Community summit was held in June 2000 (Tajikistan); report posted on http://uzland.narod.ru/2000/06_17.htm.

26. *Nezavisimaya Gazeta*, 22 October 1996, p. 3.

27. *Narodnoye Slovo*, 19 July 1999, p. 1.

28. Itar-Tass News Agency, 13 October 2000.

29. According to Martha Brill Olcott, 'Karimov ... [was] both clever enough to understand and blunt enough to state that the future of Central Asia ... [would] be determined in Moscow. At the same time ... Karimov

... [was] not eager to surrender his sovereignty to Russia.' Martha Brill Olcott, *Central Asia's New States: Independence, Foreign Policy, and Regional Security* (Washington DC: United States Institute of Peace Press, 1996), p. 136.

30. *Nezavisimaya Gazeta*, 21 June 1994, p. 1.

31. After the removal of Abdullojonov as prime minister, the Leninabadi leadership lost confidence in Emomali Rahmonov and tried to free itself, at least economically, from the rest of the republic. An extraordinary session of the Leninabad regional council voted in favour of an economic free zone, an idea that Tashkent welcomed but that was immediately rejected by Dushanbe. Oleg Panfilov, 'V khudzhande razrazilsya skandal', *Nezavisimaya Gazeta*, 30 January 1994, p. 3.

32. Itar-Tass News Agency, 20 and 22 May 1995.

33. Interfax News Agency, 16 November 1998.

34. RFE/RL, *Newsline*, 7 April 1999.

35. Xinhua News Agency, 4 February 1999.

36. RFE/RL, *Newsline*, 3 and 11 February 1999.

37. GUUAM's official webpage is available at www.guuam.org.

38. The Yalta Charter was signed on 7 June 2001. It is available online at www.ukrainaemb.lv/guuam.htm.

39. 'Uzbekistan ob´yavil o vykhode iz sostaba GUUAM', *Kommersant*, 14 June 2002.

40. On 14 June 2002 the spokesperson for the US State Department responded to questions concerning Uzbekistan's withdrawal from GUUAM by stating: 'While the organization GUUAM (Georgia, Ukraine, Uzbekistan, Azerbaijan, and Moldova) has yet to reach its full potential, we continue to believe it is a viable and promising initiative to improve regional relations and enhance cooperation among the member countries. We also believe that membership in GUUAM will help strengthen Uzbekistan's role as a regional leader, and we hope the government of Uzbekistan will reconsider its decision.' This document may be found at www.state. gov/r/pa/prs/ps/2002/11127.htm.

41. For a comprehensive account of the SCO, see Pete Lentini, 'The Shanghai Cooperation Organization and Central Asia', in Marika Vicziany, Pete Lentini and David Wright-Neville, eds, *Regional Security in the Asia Pacific: 9/11 and After* (Cheltenham: Edward Elgar, 2004), pp. 130–50. For a more optimistic assessment of the SCO's potential to contribute to regional security and state sovereignty, partly through enhance economic performance, see Gregory Gleason, 'Inter-State Cooperation in Central Asia from the CIS to the Shanghai Forum', *Europe–Asia Studies*, vol. 53, no. 7, 2001, pp. 1077–95.

42. Agence France Presse, 7 June 2002.

43. For more background reading, see Shanghai Cooperation Organization Summit – Special Press Summary: www.vic-info.org/RegionsTop.nsf/b0a93faa9a7b902f8a25682c000e4eff/cc286854507a32300a256bd10081a475?OpenDocument.

44. *Washington Post*, 23 September 2003.

45. Itar-Tass News Agency, 13 June 2002.

46. *Vremya Novostei*, 8 August 2003.
47. According to Yaacov Ro'i, 'Karimov's domestic and foreign policy have both been predicated largely on the continuance of an Islamic danger which might jeopardize his country's stability and that of the region at large.' Yaacov Ro'i, *Islam in the CIS: A Threat to Stability?* (London: Royal Institute of International Affairs, 2001), p. 56.
48. Henry Hale, 'Islam, State-building and Uzbekistan Foreign Policy', in Ali Banuazizi and Myron Weiner, eds, *The New Geopolitics of Central Asia and its Borderlands* (Bloomington and Indianapolis: Indiana University Press, 1994), p. 167.
49. Shahram Akbarzadeh, 'Uzbekistan Looks West', *Russian and Euro-Asian Bulletin*, vol. 8, no. 4, April 1999, pp. 1–8.
50. Gail W. Lapidus, 'Central Asia in Russian and American Foreign Policy after September 11, 2001', unpublished paper, presented at the University of California, Berkeley, 29 October 2001, p. 5.

4

Uzbekistan and the United States:
A Difficult Relationship

But for the dramatic collapse of the Soviet Union, Uzbekistan's entry into the international community of states would have been an uneventful episode. In March 1992 Uzbekistan joined the United Nations as its 197th member, and gradually moved to establish diplomatic representation in major capital cities. This process was hampered by the Uzbek government's lack of financial and human resources. Not surprisingly, the very first Uzbek embassy was opened in Moscow (July 1992). It was some time before other embassies could be opened, in Washington (early 1993), Bonn (October 1993) and Paris (1994). This process was an important manifestation of Uzbek sovereignty and the Uzbek leadership was proud to celebrate each occasion with fanfare. But beyond symbolism Uzbekistan faced serious limitations to its foreign policy. In the field of combating the perceived Islamic threat, the Uzbek leadership felt obliged to rely on Moscow, while it searched for a counterweight to Russia. The choice for this alternative was not difficult. The United States, the sole remaining superpower, was the ideal international partner, not only as a counterforce to Russia but as an ally against the perceived Islamic threat and as a source of financial aid and investment in Uzbekistan's dilapidated industries.

The establishment of close ties between Tashkent and Washington, however, proved to be more challenging than the Uzbek leadership had expected. While successive US administrations welcomed the emergence of the newly independent states and encouraged their integration into the global economy, three interrelated factors made Washington wary of developments in Central Asia. These concerned the absence of a strategy for democratic reforms and economic liberalisation in Uzbekistan; the perception of the absence of geostrategic assets in that region to merit US attention; and the obvious priority given to relations with Russia, which could suffer as a result of closer ties between the United States and the Central Asian states. Although the emergence of Islamic activism in Central Asia gave cause to scholars and some members of the US Congress to look at the region as important to US interests, the combination of the above three factors held the development of relations between the United States and Uzbekistan back and frustrated Uzbek overtures to Washington for a decade.

Uzbek Overtures

In the first decade of its existence as an independent state, Uzbekistan deliberately and systematically sought to align its foreign policy with that of the United States. This was particularly evident in two areas of great interest to Washington: US foreign policy towards the Middle East, especially in relation to Iran, Iraq and Israel, and the expansion of NATO membership to incorporate former Soviet satellite states.

The Middle East

Boasting about Uzbek support for US policies, the first deputy foreign minister, Sadyk Safaev, proclaimed in March 2002: 'Uzbekistan has voted 100 percent with the United States in the United Nations on controversial issues'.[1] On the sensitive question of Palestine, for example, Uzbekistan has diligently distanced itself from other Muslim states by abstaining or absenting itself from UN votes.[2] Instead Tashkent made an expression of interest in establishing diplomatic relations with Israel, a move that was warmly welcomed in Tel Aviv and Washington – but caused particular dismay in Iran. Formal ties were established in February 1992, making Uzbekistan the first Central Asian state to have such relations with Israel.[3] In subsequent years, high-level visits by Israeli statesmen to Uzbekistan and reciprocal visits by Uzbek officials to Israel consolidated bilateral ties and emphasized their common perspective on urgent regional security threats. In a 1994 visit to Tashkent the Israeli prime minister, Yitzak Rabin, and his Uzbek counterpart, Abdulhashim Mutalov, discussed the dangers posed by Islamic fundamentalism and Iran's role in sponsoring terrorism.[4]

President Karimov's visit to Israel in September 1998, the first by a Central Asian leader, offered the opportunity for both sides to reiterate their shared view of the 'Islamic threat'.[5] Israeli support for the Uzbek position was made even more clear when President Karimov received a telephone call from Israel's minister of trade and industry, Natan Sharansky, to express condolences over the February 1999 Tashkent bombing. According to the Russian news agency Itar-Tass, Sharansky expressed Israel's appreciation of 'the courage and steadfastness' that the Uzbek authorities exhibited in fighting Islamic fanatics.[6] Tashkent appeared to have found in Tel Aviv an international partner who was not cynical of its Islamophobia. Unlike the United States and members of the European Union, Israel did not criticise Tashkent for exaggerating the Islamic threat or its lack of progress in political reform. Israel's unconditional support was especially valued in Tashkent as it felt beleaguered by three distinct forces: the Islamic challenge to the legitimacy of the Uzbek leadership; Moscow's imperial ambitions; and growing pressure from the West for greater political and economic reforms. Against this backdrop, Israel's support for the Uzbek leadership and the close ties between Washington and Tel Aviv were seen in Tashkent as an opportunity to influence Washington and move towards closer ties with the United States.[7]

Another difficult issue in the Middle East that offered Tashkent an opportunity to ingratiate itself with Washington centred around Iran and its long-running dispute with the United States. Uzbekistan regarded Iran as a dangerous influence in Central Asia. Iran was seen as supporting religious fanaticism in Tajikistan and the Shiite minority in Uzbekistan. This interpretation was consistent with Washington's view of Iran as a sponsor of international terrorism. So when President Bill Clinton of the United States imposed a trade embargo on Iran in May 1995, President Karimov was prompt to endorse that policy,[8] leading to the cancellation of a planned visit to Tehran by the Uzbek foreign minister.[9] This episode caused a crisis in relations between Iran and Uzbekistan. Tashkent later denied reports of support for the embargo policy, but Uzbek–Iran relations never fully recovered.[10] Although this was not an ideal situation for Tashkent, because of the obvious limitations it placed on its regional trade options, it did offer proof of Uzbekistan's pro-US orientation in its international relations. This tendency became even more pronounced a year later. When the United Nations General Assembly took a vote on the 1996 US-held 'Iran–Libya Oil Sanctions Act', which threatened to penalise foreign companies that invested more than $40 million in the energy sectors of Iran or Libya, Uzbekistan was one of three states to stand by the United States.[11]

Tashkent's position on Iraq appeared to confirm the pattern set above. It endorsed UN-imposed sanctions and supported the role of the United States as the leading power in enforcing them. There was some confusion regarding the extent of Uzbek support for punitive air strikes on Iraq, launched by the United States and Britain in 1998 after the UN inspection team was forced to withdraw from that country. The Interfax Russian news agency quoted President Karimov as expressing dissatisfaction with US strikes because they did not enjoy UN approval.[12] However, this report may have been tainted by the official position in the Kremlin and Moscow's desire to exaggerate support for its anti-war policy. The same episode was covered by Uzbek television, with President Karimov stating that UN endorsement for the bombing raids would have been 'desirable', but that he understood why such action was taken.[13] This was a much less critical position than Interfax had suggested. In the same vein, Tashkent proved a reliable partner for the United States by signing up to the coalition of states that endorsed the US decision to go to war with Iraq in 2003, ostensibly to disarm it of weapons of mass destruction.[14] In a transparent challenge to Russia's objections, as well as those of France and Germany, President Karimov stated: 'We are concerned that some European states have a different view... if weapons of mass destruction reach the terrorists the situation will get out of control. We have had this problem for the past eleven years; this is not a problem that can be neglected any longer.'[15] Karimov justified Tashkent's support for its 'strategic partner' in relation to

Iraq by pointing to the common struggle against Islamic militancy and terrorism. The Uzbek leadership took measures to ensure that its support for US action in Iraq was not challenged in the media. According to Deutsche Welle, Uzbek media representatives were invited to meet with their foreign minister in March 2003 and were told to cover the war by relying on US sources. They were specifically instructed not to give airtime to the Russian anti-war position.[16] But unconfirmed reports from Uzbekistan suggest that Tashkent's official line and conspicuous alignment with the United States in the region did not correspond to the general sentiment among Uzbeks, especially in the Ferghana Valley.[17]

NATO

Plans for the eastward expansion of NATO in the 1990s offered Tashkent a highly visible and significant issue to use in its overtures to Washington. Tashkent presented itself as Washington's natural ally in the process of de-Sovietisation. It unequivocally rejected Moscow's objections to the admission of East European states to NATO as misguided and dangerous. In the same vein, Tashkent dismissed Russian ambitions to turn the CIS into a military alliance as a counterweight to NATO. President Karimov warned, ominously, that the realisation of Russia's ambitions for the CIS would turn the clock back and return CIS members to the past.[18]

Uzbekistan maintained that former Soviet satellite states should be treated as sovereign and criticised residual Russian imperial aspirations for placing external pressure on their foreign policy. Meeting with the visiting US defense secretary, William Perry, for example, President Karimov expressed concern about 'the voices of imperialism in Russia and the ever louder utterances of nostalgia'.[19] Karimov impressed upon the defense secretary that Uzbekistan viewed NATO as offering a gateway to regional stability and security for the former Soviet bloc. Accordingly the president was supportive of Czech ambitions to join NATO, when visiting Prague in January 1997.[20] In a subsequent interview, President Karimov stated that far from being a threat to CIS security, as projected by the Russian top brass, NATO's expansion represented the spread of international peace.[21]

Uzbekistan's pro-NATO position was an irritant for Russia, undermining its geopolitical strategy. In April 1999, when Moscow was trying to create a united front against the NATO operation in Yugoslavia, Uzbekistan deliberately distanced itself from Russia and refused to sign a declaration against NATO bombings. The eventual document signed by all CIS presidents amounted to a muted call for the cessation of hostilities and bloodshed in Kosovo.[22] This call fell short of Moscow's expectations and an earlier statement which had been signed by defence ministers of Russia, Armenia, Tajikistan, Belarus and Kyrgyzstan. This statement (25 March) had condemned NATO air-strikes against Yugoslavia as 'inhuman' and 'a threat to peace and security', which violated 'norms of international law'.[23] This disagreement provided the background to Tashkent's official step away from Moscow. At the April 1999 summit, Uzbekistan announced that it would not renew its membership in the CIS CST.

Uzbekistan's pro-NATO orientation was made public in 1994, when it joined the outer periphery of NATO by signing up for the NATO Partnership for Peace (PfP) programme.[24] The significance of this move was overshadowed by the open-door policy of that programme and Russia's association with NATO, announced in the same year. Nevertheless, Tashkent was determined to affirm its relations with NATO beyond symbolism. In 1995 Uzbekistan, along with Kyrgyzstan and Kazakhstan formed the Central Asian Battalion (Centrazbat) as a peacekeeping force within the framework of NATO PfP and took part in a joint military exercise with US troops.[25] Subsequent US/Centrazbat exercises were held in 1997, 1998 and 2000 in Central Asia. Uzbekistan was not present at the March 2001 training camps in Nova Scotia (Canada), but the Uzbek leadership has been at pains to emphasise its commitment to close security relations with the United States and its allies. At a press conference in 1999, for example, President Karimov declared his enthusiasm for close military ties with Turkey because of that country's full NATO membership and the benefits that Turkish–Uzbek relations would offer Uzbekistan's closer ties with NATO.[26]

The US Response

The US administration was ambivalent in its response to Uzbek overtures. Washington welcomed the emergence of the newly independent states and moved quickly to establish diplomatic relations with them.

The United States recognised Uzbekistan on 25 December 1991, and established diplomatic relations with Tashkent on 19 February 1992. The US embassy in Uzbekistan was opened on 16 March 1992. But concern with human rights issues and Russia impeded the evolution of US–Uzbek relations beyond diplomatic niceties. The absence of democratic reforms in Uzbekistan was particularly irritating for the Democratic administration of President Bill Clinton, which held office for a good part of Uzbekistan's first decade of independence. According to the US ambassador to Uzbekistan, Stanley Escudero, as much as Washington valued relations with Tashkent the question of democratic reforms could not be ignored.[27] On the contrary, the United States in this period consistently worked to promote political openness and reforms through high-level lobbying of the Uzbek leadership and sponsoring various civil society initiatives to encourage NGOs. Ambassador Escudero made a direct reference to his office's efforts to encourage the registration of the Birlik opposition party.

It is revealing to note that President Islam Karimov made his first visit to the White House in June 1996 – five years after independence.[28] This visit did not proceed smoothly. President Bill Clinton was initially reported to have declined a face-to-face meeting with Karimov due to Uzbekistan's poor human rights record. But the two presidents managed to have a brief session, only made possible by the granting of a presidential pardon to eighty-nine political prisoners in Uzbekistan on the eve of President Karimov's trip to the United States.[29] Subsequent reports, however, suggested that only five prisoners were actually released.[30] In contrast with the cool nature of this presidential encounter, President Karimov was greeted warmly in the Pentagon, where he met US Secretary of Defense William Perry and discussed security issues in Central Asia and prospects of bilateral cooperation in the field of military training and Uzbekistan's role in the NATO PfP.[31] William Perry was quoted as praising Uzbekistan at this meeting as an 'island of stability' in the region.[32] The contrast between these two episodes epitomised the difficulties faced by the US administration in running two parallel foreign-policy agendas in relation to Central Asia: regional security and democratisation.

The US policy towards Central Asia was also informed by that region's vast reserves of oil and gas. In fact access to these energy reserves appeared to be the most compelling and indisputable reason for Washington's interest in Central Asia. In February 1998 Assistant Secretary of State Robert Gee set out US interests in the region before the House Committee on International Relations, Sub-Committee on Asia and the Pacific. These were energy security, geostrategic interests and commercial.[33] Gee expounded that finding multiple export routes for oil and gas from the Caspian basin region was critical for its integration into the world economy. It would also diversify sources of energy and reduce current dependence on the Persian Gulf region's oil and gas, and challenge the ability of any state to monopolise export routes. Although this policy was presented as 'not intended to bypass or to thwart Russia', the East–West energy corridor across the Caspian Sea favoured by the Clinton administration had that effect, and Washington could not but have been aware of this outcome. Perhaps in an effort to exonerate itself from the charge of threatening Russia's interests in its 'backyard', the administration was prepared to refrain from taking a salient role in Central Asia. Instead it put its trust in market forces and the private sector, or what Stephen Blank has termed 'dollar diplomacy',[34] to achieve its objectives: 'we have always maintained that commercial considerations will first and foremost determine the outcome [of alternative pipelines].'[35] In another public hearing, Assistant Secretary of State Marc Grossman echoed Gee and set out US goals in the region as 'promoting development, increasing trade, strengthening market economies, and avoiding conflict'.[36]

Yet this one-dimensional approach to Central Asia was untenable. The United States was gradually becoming concerned with the emergence of Islamic militancy in Central Asia, and its regional and global implications. At the same time a growing body of US scholars and policy advisers were expressing misgivings about what they saw as shortcomings in the Clinton administration's policy towards Central Asia. These misgivings primarily targeted the exaggerated importance of Russia in the administration's thinking, which tended to overshadow other regions and their importance to the United States. The tone was set by Paul Wolfowitz, dean of the School of Advanced International Studies at Johns Hopkins University, and a former defense undersecretary in the Bush (senior) administration. Writing in the influential journal *Foreign Affairs* in 1994, Wolfowitz argued against subordinating US interests in the former Soviet bloc to US–Russia relations. A 'Russia first' policy, which ignored Russia's failure to steer a moderate and democratic course, was at risk of 'slipping into a dangerous and misguided policy of "Russia only"'.[37] This point was echoed four years later by Frederick Starr in his congressional testimony: 'too often over the past six years we have viewed policy towards Central Asia and the Caspian basin as a sub-set of some other policy concern, usually Russia, rather than a focus of American policy in its own right.'[38]

A consensus view was emerging among a body of foreign-policy think-tanks and regional experts regarding the importance of Central Asia to US interests. Perhaps the most influential was Zbigniew Brzezinski, national security adviser to President Jimmy Carter between 1977 and 1981, and professor of American foreign policy at the School of Advanced International Studies, Johns Hopkins University.[39] Brzezinski took issue with the 'grand strategy' of the Clinton administration, labelling it 'idealistic optimism'. He argued that placing the primary focus of US relations with Russia turned a blind eye to areas of incompatibility of interests in regard to Russia's southern neighbours, and risked ignoring Moscow's imperial impulses. Instead he argued for a much more proactive US policy towards Central Asia that was not bound by fears of Russian reaction, or the slow pace of democratic reforms in that region. In his assessment, US strategic interests were paramount:

> US political relations with Uzbekistan, and to some extent Turkmenistan, both of which appear determined to resist external domination, have lagged behind because in Washington's view these largely Muslim countries have made insufficient progress toward democracy. Yet US policy toward Kuwait or Saudi Arabia, for example, does not appear to be motivated by the same concern and, for equally good strategic reasons, neither was it in years past toward Taiwan or Korea.[40]

This 'realist' push to free US policy on Central Asia from ideological constraints was gaining momentum in the mid-1990s. The Washington-based School of Advanced International Studies at Johns Hopkins University appeared to be a driving force in challenging the Clinton administration's neglect of Central Asia. This was made possible by the extensive experience of its professors in forming US foreign policy and the links they maintained with various government agencies. Both Wolfowitz and Brzezinski, mentioned above, had worked in the previous administration and were widely known for advocating an assertive foreign policy.[41]

The School's role became even more salient in 1996 when it launched its Central Asia–Caucasus Institute, under the directorship of Frederick Starr. In a series of public lectures by top US officials and visiting dignitaries from the region, the Institute was instrumental in highlighting the strategic importance of Central Asia and the Caucasus for the administration. In July 1997, for example, the Institute hosted Deputy Secretary Strobe Talbott. His address was important on two counts. It signalled the administration's growing interest in the Central Asia republics; the United States, Talbott proposed, had a 'stake in their success' as independent states.[42] But this interest was conditional. US interest in Central Asia was part of the broader approach to Russia and the process of democratisation. Talbott's address indicated a clear shift in the administration's assessment of Central Asia and its importance. But this was an incremental shift, kept in check by other considerations. The Institute was keen to accelerate this shift.

Immediately before becoming chair of the new Institute, Starr published an article in *Foreign Affairs* on the regional dynamics of Central Asia and identified Uzbekistan as the state with the appropriate population, resources, geography and leadership to make it pivotal to regional stability, hence making that state important to the US.[43] In Starr's assessment, Uzbekistan was 'uniquely positioned to anchor the security of the region'.[44] The idea of Uzbekistan as an anchor state found resonance in Brzezinski's thinking on the matter. Promulgating a new 'geostrategy for Eurasia', he argued for Uzbekistan to be given the weight it was due in US foreign policy. Uzbekistan was a 'strategically pivotal' state, Brzezinski insisted, and closer relations between the United States and that former Soviet republic would not only allow the US to have a role in making Central Asia stable but also 'temper any residual Russian imperial temptations'.[45]

Winds of Change

These calls were not in vain. The Clinton administration was gradually adjusting its policy toward Uzbekistan in recognition of that state's geostrategic importance, especially in regard to the emerging threat of international terrorism from Afghanistan. According to the *Washington Post*, the August 1998 terrorist attacks by al-Qaeda on US embassies in Kenya and Tanzania were the catalyst that brought Washington and Tashkent together.[46] It was reported that the CIA used a secret presidential 'finding' to develop ties with the Uzbek secret service, presumably to exchange intelligence. There were also unconfirmed reports that Washington was planning to use Uzbek territory to launch an air attack on al-Qaeda training camps in Afghanistan.[47] Perhaps the single event that highlighted Uzbekistan's importance for the Clinton administration in its ongoing security campaign against terrorist groups in Central Asia and Afghanistan was the August 2000 taking hostage of four American mountain climbers by the IMU. The hostages managed to escape their captors, but it was no longer possible for Washington to ignore the IMU or Uzbekistan. The US State Department's classification of the IMU as a terrorist organisation following this incident offered implicit support to Tashkent. This move was enthusiastically welcomed by the Uzbek leadership, which felt vindicated in its fight against Islamists.

The US administration was still uncomfortable with dropping or downplaying its objections to Uzbekistan's abysmal human rights record and the absence of political reforms, and neglecting Russian sensitivities. But the US Congress appeared to be less constrained by such ideological concerns and more interested in 'expert advice'. At the third hearing on the Caspian Sea region held by the Subcommittee on International Economic Policy, Export and Trade Promotion of the Committee on Foreign Relations, senators heard from two prominent experts in this field: Zbigniew Brzezinski and Martha Brill Olcott. Both emphasised the long-term importance of Central Asia to US interests. Brzezinski stressed the danger of Balkanisation, 'namely a region of internal weakness, internal instability, internal ethnic, national, or religious conflicts'.[48] According to Brzezinski, such a scenario would not only affect the neighbouring states; it would also have implications for the United States. The geostrategic importance of Central Asia, he contended, lay in its rich energy resources and minerals. Brzezinski concluded his testimony by reiterating his earlier call for a comprehensive policy towards the region, now choosing to quote the subcommittee chair Senator Chuck Hagel (R): 'The United States must put forward a clear, comprehensive, and effective

US policy for this region, particularly for the development of a western route for Caspian Sea oil.'

This testimony was followed by that of Martha Brill Olcott, who presented a less economically inclined account. While acknowledging the importance of Central Asian resources for the United States, Olcott chose to focus on the critical role of Uzbekistan for regional stability. Olcott contended that Uzbekistan had in place the most 'effective security force' capable of handling sporadic unrest in that country; but in case of large-scale social unrest the Uzbek regime would be ill-prepared. In such a scenario, she argued, internal social strife in Uzbekistan would 'inevitably lead to spill-over' of unrest to neighbouring Central Asian republics. Although Olcott refrained from drawing normative conclusions regarding the nature of relations between the United States and Uzbekistan, these were self-evident. If the United States was interested in preserving regional stability and promoting Central Asia's economic integration into the global market, as everyone at the hearing deemed desirable, then it would be imperative to cultivate relations between Tashkent and Washington and strengthen Uzbekistan as an anchor state.

Only a few months after this hearing, the Senate approved the Security Assistance Act of 1998 to offer defence articles and services to a number of former Soviet republics, among them Uzbekistan. This was followed by the Senate adoption of the Silk Road Strategy Act of 1998, which envisioned US assistance principally to the development of transport infrastructure and energy-extracting industries, as well as human rights and democratic governance. This Act was first drafted in 1997 and had a strong commercial and security orientation. It stipulated that the United States should

- Assist the region in developing intra-regional economic cooperation and friendly relations which may stabilize the Caspian Basin and help fortify the area against future conflict;
- Support US strategic and commercial interests by providing urgently needed economic, technical and financial assistance, as well as help with the development of telecommunications and transportation infrastructures in Azerbaijan and other nations in the region;
- Provide security-related assistance in the form of military education, counter-proliferation training and surplus U.S. military equipment and supplies;
- Encourage democratic and free-market institutions.[49]

The adoption of this bill entrenched the inevitable shift in perceptions of Central Asia and the recognition of its importance to the United States. It also foreshadowed the move away from the Clinton administration's concern with human rights as a determining factor in relations between Washington and Central Asia. In his report, Senator Helms from the Committee on Foreign Relations proclaimed:

> It is necessary to recognize that human rights problems exist in every country in the region. Under existing human rights statutes however, the Administration has not found such violations to be sufficient to merit a cut-off of US assistance.[50]

Security concerns for the United States could not be ignored. It was revealing that the US Army commissioned a study of risks to regional stability in Central Asia and the South Caucasus during Bill Clinton's presidency.[51] This study was largely completed before the September 11 attacks and the sudden reorientation of US policy towards Central Asia. The study, which was finally published in 2003, revealed that even in the Democratic administration there was a growing realisation that the US could no longer ignore the security threats emanating from Russia's former Muslim colonies. A policy shift towards Central Asia was in the making. This shift was buoyed by an academic publication in January 2001, coinciding with the change in the US presidency. The *Strategic Assessment of Central Asia*, produced jointly by the Atlantic Council of the United States and the Central Asia–Caucasus Institute at Johns Hopkins University, presented the most comprehensive and documented argument for the relevance of Central Asia to the regional and global interests of the United States. The authors, among them Frederick Starr, argued forcefully that geographic distance should not blind foreign-policy-makers to the strategic importance of the region.[52]

Conclusion

Given the trajectory of foreign-policy thinking in the 1990s, described in this chapter, it was logical to expect that the ascendency of the Republican leadership under President George W. Bush would consolidate the new approach towards Central Asia. In the early months of 2001 the shift away from ideological concerns with human rights and political openness seemed inevitable. But no one could foresee the accelerated pace of the change. The 11 September 2001 attacks on the United States and the subsequent 'war on terror' made Central Asia integral to Washington's global security agenda. More than ever before, Washington sees an organic connection between security for the United States at home and abroad. The paramountcy of the security agenda has freed the Bush administration from the constraints that impeded the United States in Central Asia during the first decade of its independence. Concerns about alienating Russia by 'encroaching' on its backyard, or appearing to endorse authoritarian regimes by establishing closer ties with the Central Asian states, have been superseded by security objectives. This new development could not suit the Uzbek leadership better. The coalescence of US and Uzbek interests, explored in the next chapter, was accelerated exponentially beyond anything President Karimov could imagine.

Notes

1. EurasiaNet, 'Q&A with Uzbek Deputy Foreign First Minister Sadyk Safaev', 11 March 2002, posted on www.uzland.uz/2002/march/13/03.htm.
2. Uzbekistan was absent from voting on UN resolutions A/RES/57/110: Peaceful Settlement of the Question of Palestine (adopted by the General Assembly on 3 December 2002) and A/RES/57/111: Jerusalem (adopted by the General Assembly on 3 December 2002). Uzbekistan abstained on resolution A/RES/57/112: The Syrian Golan (adopted by the General Assembly on 3 December 2002). See United Nations Dag Hammarskjöld Library, UNBISnet – Voting Records. A similar voting pattern is evident in relation to UN resolutions against the US embargo on trade with Cuba. In annual UN General Assembly votes, only Uzbekistan, Israel and the United States systematically vote against lifting the ban on Cuba.
3. Voice of Israel, 22 February 1992, cited in BBC Summary of World Broadcasts, 24 February 1992.
4. BBC News, 20 December 1994.
5. Agence France Presse, 14 September 1998.
6. Itar-Tass News Agency, 18 February 1999.
7. According to a Russian commentator, 'Uzbeks want to make their peace with America through Israel.' See *Izvestiya*, 5 July 1994, p. 3.
8. Associated Press, 4 May 1995.
9. United Press International, 12 May 1995.
10. Itar-Tass News Agency, 19 May 1995.

11. Israel, Micronesia, the United States and Uzbekistan voted against the resolution, which was adopted with 56 in favour, 76 abstentions and 4 against. Inter Press Service, 29 November 1996.
12. Interfax, 18 December 1998.
13. Uzbek Television first channel, 18 December 1998, cited in BBC Summary of World Broadcasts, 22 December 1998.
14. Associated Press, 21 March 2003.
15. Viktoria Panfilova, 'Moskva za nami, Gosudarstva Tsentral'noi Azii stali tsentrom mezhdunarodnykh intrig', *Nezavisimaya Gazeta*, 14 March 2003.
16. Deutsche Welle, 20 March 2003.
17. Igor Rotar, *Izvestiya*, 10 April 2003.
18. United Press International, 27 December 1996.
19. Deutsche Presse-Agentur, 6 April 1995.
20. Associated Press, 16 January 1997.
21. *Kommersant-Daily*, 28 March 1997, p. 3.
22. RFE/RL, *Newsline*, 6 April 1999.
23. RFE/RL, *Newsline*, 26 March 1999.
24. www.nato.int/pfp/sig-cntr.htm.
25. For a useful account of Uzbekistan's military cooperation with the United States, see Kenley Butler, 'U.S. Military Cooperation with the Central Asian States', at cns.miis.edu/research/wtco1/uscamil.htm.
26. BBC Monitoring, 'Uzbek and Turkish Presidents Give Press Conference', 19 March 1999.
27. *Nezavisimaya Gazeta*, 8 August 1996, p. 3.
28. Annette Bohr, *Uzbekistan: Politics and Foreign Policy* (London: Royal Institute of International Affairs, 1998), p. 65.
29. *Nezavisimaya Gazeta*, 22 June 1996, p. 3.
30. RFE/RL, *Newsline*, 26 June 1996.
31. Department of Defense, Memorandum no. 144–M, 26 June 1996. Federal Document Clearing House.
32. S. Frederick Starr, 'Making Eurasia Stable', *Foreign Affairs*, vol. 74, no. 1, January–February 1996, p. 92.
33. Federal News Service, 12 February 1998.
34. Stephen Blank, 'The United States and Central Asia', in Roy Allison and Lena Jonson, eds, *Central Asian Security: The New International Context* (Washington DC: Brookings Institution Press, 2001), p. 139.
35. Robert W. Gee before the House Committee on International Relations, Federal News Service, 12 February 1998.
36. Marc Grossman, Assistant Secretary of State for European and Canadian Affairs, before the Senate Foreign Relations Committee, Sub-Committee on International Economic Policy, Export, and Trade Promotion. Federal News Service, 8 July 1998.
37. Paul D. Wolfowitz, 'Clinton's First Year', *Foreign Affairs*, vol. 73, no. 1, January–February 1994, p. 41.
38. S. Frederick Starr before the House Committee on International Relations, Sub-Committee on Asia and the Pacific, Federal News Service, 12 February 1998.

39. Zbigniew Brzezinski, 'The Premature Partnership', *Foreign Affairs*, vol. 73, no. 2, March–April 1994, pp. 67–83.

40. Ibid., p. 67.

41. Paul Wolfowitz later joined the administration of President George W. Bush in 2001 as the deputy defense secretary, under the hawkish Donald Rumsfeld.

42. Deputy Secretary Talbott, address at the Johns Hopkins School of Advanced International Studies, Baltimore, Maryland, 21 July 1997, www.state. gov.

43. Starr, 'Making Eurasia Stable', pp. 80–92.

44. Ibid., p. 85.

45. Zbigniew Brzezinski, 'A Geostrategy for Eurasia', *Foreign Affairs*, vol. 76, no. 5, September–October 1997, p. 57.

46. *Washington Post*, 14 October 2001, p. A01.

47. See, for example, Ahmed Rashid, 'US Seeks Alliance with Moscow for Raid on Bin Laden', *Daily Telegraph*, 22 November 2000.

48. 'Implementation Of U.S. Policy on Caspian Sea Oil Exports', hearing before the Subcommittee on International Economic Policy, Export and Trade Promotion of the Committee on Foreign Relations, United States Senate, 105th Congress, Second Session, 8 July 1998, www.access.gpo. gov/congress/senate.

49. Center for Security Policy, 'Caspian Watch #8: "Silk Road" Legislation Opens New Opportunities for US Strategic, Commercial Interests in the Caspian Basin', *Decision Brief*, No. 97–D157, 23 September 1997.

50. United States Senate, 105th Congress, Second Session, 9 October 1998, www.access.gpo.gov/congress/senate.

51. Olga Oliker and Thomas S. Szayna, eds, *Faultlines of Conflict in Central Asia and the South Caucasus* (Santa Monica, CA: Rand, 2003).

52. Charles Fairbanks, S. Frederick Starr, C. Richard Nelson and Kenneth Weisbrode, *Strategic Assessment of Central Asia* (Washington, DC: Atlantic Council of the United States, and Central Asia–Caucasus Institute, SAIS, Johns Hopkins University, 2001).

5

September 11 and the
'War on Terror'

The September 11 attacks changed the way Central Asia was perceived in US foreign policy. Uzbekistan was suddenly thrust onto the international scene as the staging ground in the 'war on terror'. The large-scale military operation that was launched on 7 October 2001 against the Taliban brought over 5,000 American soldiers to Central Asia, stationed in Kyrgyzstan, Tajikistan and Uzbekistan. This deployment of US forces to Russia's backyard was justified as a tactical move, essential for the successful conduct of the war in Afghanistan. But, as discussed in the previous chapter, a discernable trend towards recognising Uzbekistan's significance as a regional player and a potential partner had preceded this rapid shift. The 'war on terror' was the expediting factor for an already existing trend.

President Islam Karimov was acutely aware of the window of opportunity that September 11 offered Uzbek relations with the United States. He was among the first leaders to send a message of sympathy and solidarity to President George W. Bush. This message was reinforced by a separate statement by Uzbekistan's foreign minister, who declared that Tashkent would carefully study any request for assistance from Washington in the campaign against Islamic extremists and the Taliban.[1] Within a fortnight some 200 US soldiers arrived at a military airport near Tashkent.[2] This deployment took place amid conflicting reports about the extent of Uzbekistan's involvement in the impending operation in Afghanistan. President Karimov had denied giving US forces access to Uzbekistan's airspace or territory for the purpose of military action against the Taliban.[3] Even after the arrival of the first deployment, Uzbek authorities refrained from confirming such reports. Only on 1 October 2001 did the Uzbek Security Council under the chairmanship of President Karimov publicly announce that Tashkent would open its airspace to the United States.[4] Despite the conspicuous omission of any reference to the Khanabad airbase in this statement, it was widely known that Tashkent was allowing the use of that base, some 500 kilometres from Tashkent, by American forces.

Addressing the Tashkent city council two weeks after the September 11 attacks, President Karimov expressed deep indignation at this barbarous act and emphasised that Uzbeks have also suffered at the hands of the terrorists.[5] This was a familiar proclamation for his audience, one that had been repeatedly used to define the nature of the relationship between the Uzbek regime and its political opponents. The significance of this statement was in its timing and its intended audience well beyond those present at the city hall. Karimov was addressing three distinct groups.

- His domestic audience was uneasy about Uzbekistan's involvement in a military assault on a Muslim neighbour. For them, Karimov reiterated Bush's assurances that this was a war not on Islam, but on extremism and barbarity. This message was reinforced systematically by visiting US officials who made sure to include the Islamic clergy on their list of people to meet.
- His American audience needed to be assured that Uzbekistan was a reliable partner, as it had gone through the same experience with Islamic terrorists and shared a common objective with Washington. As far as Tashkent was concerned, this partnership was long overdue.
- The message for his Russian audience was mixed. Karimov presented the decision to join the US-led operation as a fait accompli and not open to negotiation. At the same time, this was an object-specific commitment, not an open-ended invitation to host US forces in Uzbekistan. This, it might be argued, was intended to calm the anxiety that Tashkent's position had caused in Moscow.

This chapter examines the rapid evolution of the US–Uzbek partnership and its implications for Russia's relations with Uzbekistan.

US–Uzbek Partnership

Uzbekistan offered an important point of access to Afghanistan, and Washington was eager to secure Tashkent's commitment to the anti-terrorist coalition. This allowed Tashkent to position itself as a key player in the campaign, with two obvious objectives: eliminating the Islamic threat posed by the Taliban and the IMU, which was taking refuge in Afghanistan; and proving itself as a reliable partner for the United States beyond that immediate operation. This position was acknowledged by the Bush administration on several occasions, the most diplomatic and sensitive one being at a meeting between the US ambassador, John Herbst, and the staff members of the office of the muftiyat in Tashkent.[6] The importance of Uzbekistan's role was also made clear by Donald Rumsfeld in a visit in November 2001, during which he praised Uzbekistan's cooperation and indicated the shift in Washington's assessment of the Central Asian republic.[7] Unlike his predecessor, William Perry, on his trip to Uzbekistan in April 1995 Rumsfeld did not raise human rights as a point of discussion and confined official talks to urgent arrangements for Uzbekistan's involvement in the Afghanistan campaign.

Within six months of the commencement of the US-led operation in Afghanistan, the Taliban were driven out of power.[8] This operation was presented by the Bush administration as a battle between good and evil. The Taliban and al-Qaeda represented Islamic extremism and barbarity, while the United States and its allies represented civilisation and decency. This dichotomy was quite familiar to the Uzbek regime as it had consistently labelled its opponents, especially the IMU and Hizb ut-Tahrir, as murderous and evil. Now the remaining superpower seemed to be using Karimov's terminology against a common enemy. This could not but hearten the Uzbek leadership.

The stationing of US forces in Khanabad, which at times numbered around 5,000, was seen in Tashkent as a potent symbol of Uzbekistan's new-found importance to the United States. US forces had also established a presence in Tajikistan and Kyrgyzstan. But Uzbekistan was seen as the linchpin of the American anti-Taliban campaign from the north. This understanding was formalised in March 2002 when Uzbekistan and the United States signed a Declaration on Strategic Partnership.[9] The agreement confirmed Washington's commitment to Uzbekistan's security and territorial integrity; in return Tashkent reaffirmed its pledge of support for the US-led 'war on terror'. Other agreements in conjunction with the 'strategic partnership' included a nuclear non-proliferation programme to replace highly enriched uranium from an Uzbek research reactor with lower-grade material; a US$55m credit from the US Export–Import Bank to small and medium-sized Uzbek enterprises for the purchase of US goods; and further cooperation in the field of science and technology.[10]

The signing of the Strategic Partnership was described by President George W. Bush as opening a 'new chapter' in US–Uzbek relations.[11] The Uzbek government could not agree more. *Watanparvar*, published by the Uzbek army, praised the partnership as offering 'unlimited opportunities and inexhaustible potential'. The newspaper continued: 'The partnership raises economic, political, social, cultural, military and technical cooperation to a new, unprecedented height, strengthening Uzbekistan's international stance for the promotion of peace and stability in the region, guaranteeing peaceful life, well-being and prosperity for our nation.'[12] This assessment, exaggerated as it sounds, appeared to be supported by an official visit from the US Senate. The Uzbek government gloated about the arrival of a US Senate delegation led by Senator Richard Shelby, deputy chairman of the Senate Intelligence Committee, in Tashkent less than two weeks from the signing of the Strategic Partnership Declaration. A state-controlled daily claimed that this visit was evidence of fast-expanding relations between Uzbekistan and the United States. It further claimed that these bilateral achievements illustrated that the 'world community' has taken notice of President Karimov's leadership and 'constructive reforms'.[13]

By the end of 2002, Uzbekistan was firmly entrenched in the mind of the US administration as a dependable ally. Some referred to it as a 'leading' state in Central Asia,[14] giving credence to the idea that Uzbekistan has gained a special relationship with the United States whereby Washington tacitly approved Tashkent's hegemonic aspirations in return for gaining a foothold in the region to protect its commercial and security interests. This is precisely what the Uzbek leadership sought – an important factor that explains the level of official jubilation at the formalisation of US–Uzbek partnership against Islamism.

Many observers have commented that the advent of cosy relations between the United States and Uzbekistan is likely to have a detrimental impact on the latter's move away from authoritarianism and on the protection of human rights.[15] President Karimov himself was aware of this view and moved to placate such concerns by initiating the inclusion of his government's commitment to 'democratic reforms' in the terms of the US–Uzbek Strategic Partnership. Nonetheless, misgivings among human rights groups have not been pacified. In an editorial, written at the height of the 'war on terror' in Afghanistan, the Washington Post argued that the December 2001 meeting between Secretary of State Colin Powell and President Karimov sent the wrong message to other Central Asian rulers: 'If you play ball with the United States in Afghanistan we will look the other way as a decade of democratization efforts is ground to dust.'[16] Uzbekistan's human rights record continues to be a point of contention in Washington.

The US administration is, of course, aware of the widespread view that democratisation is being sacrificed for security and does not wish to be seen as fulfilling it. The United States cannot afford to be seen as completely giving up on the promotion of political openness and reforms.

In June 2002 Lynn Pascoe, US deputy assistant secretary of state, visiting Tashkent for the third time in six months, rejected as 'totally false' fears that the US interest in cooperating with the Uzbek government in fighting terrorism would overshadow efforts to promote democracy and market reforms in Uzbekistan. 'As we increase the connections between us at all levels ... it is absolutely critical that progress be made on economic and political reform.'[17] In the same breath, he added: 'we perfectly well know that this sort of change sometimes takes time.' Implicit in the last concession on the pace of reforms was the acceptance of the Uzbek leadership's commitment to political and economic openness at face value. This was consistent with Colin Powell's 'candid discussion' with President Karimov in December 2001, when he stated: 'President Karimov wants to bring through a new generation that understands democracy. It is the pace of democratisation that is on his mind.'[18] The tone of the secretary of state was discernibly more accommodating than his predecessor, Madeleine Albright. On an official visit to Tashkent the previous year,

Albright warned of political radicalisation in the absence of demo-cratic reforms: 'indiscriminate government censorship and repression can cause moderate and peaceful opponents of a regime to resort to violence.'[19] There was no such warning in Colin Powell's 'candid' exchange with President Karimov. Instead Powell was giving voice to the position long advocated by scholars at the School of Advanced International Studies at Johns Hopkins University, and authors of the *Strategic Assessment of Central Asia*, discussed in the previous chapter.

This position was further expanded by Powell's assistant secretary of state, Elizabeth Jones, when she addressed an academic conference at the University of Montana Missoula (April 2003). According to Jones, 'the United States is wholly committed to intensive engage-ment and dialogue' with the countries of Central Asia:

> Our disengagement from Afghanistan in the 1980s taught us a harsh lesson, one that we do not want to repeat in other countries. We learned that we must engage the region's governments and people to promote long-term stability and prevent a security vacuum that provides opportuni-ties for extremism and external intervention. This is particularly true in Georgia, Uzbekistan, Kyrgyzstan and Tajikistan, where terrorist groups have threatened our own national interests.[20]

As argued earlier, the United States cannot afford to be seen as sacrificing the human rights agenda. The US State Department has retained Uzbekistan in the list of countries of concern for their violation of basic freedoms, including religious freedom and human rights. Following reports of torture and death in custody, the visiting US assistant secretary of the State Department, Lorne Cramer, told reporters in Tashkent that 'further expansion of bilateral relations is contingent on improvements in Uzbekistan's human rights record'.[21] But this assertion appears to be a residual policy line from the pre-September 11 era. The accelerated expansion of relations on issues of security, and Uzbekistan's access to funds from the United States and other international sources, indicate that concern with politi-cal reform would not be allowed to dictate the terms of bilateral relations. A more accurate assessment was presented by a middle-ranking official at the US embassy in Kazakhstan, who argued that unfavourable reports on Uzbekistan's human rights record by the US State Department were intended for internal use, not as a 'stick for hitting anyone'.[22]

As a consequence of Uzbekistan's role in the US-led coalition, Tashkent has enjoyed an unprecedented boost in US aid and economic assistance. In December 2002 a high-ranking US official announced that the United States would recommend a reconstruction loan from the IMF to help reform and rebuild Uzbek industries. It was clear that the United States planned to reward Uzbekistan for its loyalty. According to the State Department, 'in FY2002, US Government assistance to Uzbekistan increased almost fourfold, from approximately US$85 million in FY 2001 to almost US$300 million in FY2002.'[23] This was substantially higher than aid to other Central Asian states; the second highest recipient of US aid, Tajikistan, received US$162 million in FY2002, while Kyrgyzstan was granted US$114 million in assistance. These funds were earmarked for security programmes, humanitarian assistance and cross-sectoral initiatives (such as water management and health care reform). In addition to the above, various state agencies offer Uzbekistan financial and in-kind assistance. For example, in July 2002 the US Trade and Development Agency committed US$3.5 million to assist various projects involving information technology, power and water resources development, as well as a delivery of military hospital equipment to the value of US$15 million.[24]

It is noteworthy that the new strategic alignment between Uzbekistan and the United States against Islamism has been interpreted as the ticket for closer security cooperation between the UK and Uzbekistan. Unconfirmed reports suggest that in December 2001 London approved the unlimited sale of arms to Uzbekistan and other Central Asian states hosting US troops. In 2002 arms sales amounted to more than £34 million. News of arms deals has led the British media to accuse the government of Tony Blair of supporting authoritarian states and sacrificing human rights at the altar of the 'war on terror'.[25]

Handling Russian Concerns

The formalisation of the US–Uzbek strategic partnership offered Tashkent an opportunity to make a long-sought readjustment in its relations with Moscow. President Karimov was a vocal critic of

Russia's imperial 'hangover' in relation to Central Asia and, as with Uzbek–Tajik relations, was frustrated by the way its neighbours kowtowed to Moscow. But the arrival of the United States on the scene and the subsequent relationship that evolved between Tashkent and Washington have emboldened the Uzbek leadership. They show no inhibition in the way they reject Russia's objections to the new strategic realities in Central Asia. For example, President Karimov, responding to reports that Moscow asked to be consulted before Tashkent decided to allow US troops onto Uzbek soil, stated that Russian leaders 'do not like the fact that Uzbekistan is carrying out its own independent policy.... But let me say once again that when the Soviet army invaded Afghanistan in 1979, starting a big war, no one asked for our approval.'[26] According to Karimov, Russia only offered 'vague promises' to fight Islamic terrorism in the late 1990s when Tashkent sought international assistance to combat the IMU, whereas the United States delivered on its promise; and Tashkent was not going to forget that disparity. In an interview, Karimov publicly mocked Russia for its inability to lead the CIS Collective Security Treaty in an effective campaign against Islamists:

> In CIS structures we talked, created quick reaction detachments, signed agreements and thousands of documents, etc. [But] practically, it was the United States and its coalition that destroyed terrorist bases in Afghanistan. It is pointless to make oneself seem important. We should consider who played which part and who played the main role. I say that the United States played a decisive role [with] their determination, the exemplary professionalism of their soldiers and level of their armaments. Everybody else played secondary roles.[27]

This new boost to Uzbek self-confidence has given Russian leaders more cause for concern, to the extent that Russian analysts and commentators openly question President Vladimir Putin's coy position in relation to the American force deployment in Central Asia. According to the Russian daily *Nezavisimaya Gazeta*, the arrival of every American soldier in Uzbekistan chips away at Russia's influence in the region.[28] This concern was shared by many Russian deputies in the Duma where a motion was put to the vote, condemning the US presence in Uzbekistan at the height of the military campaign against the Taliban. This motion was convincingly defeated, but it still received 136 votes from 38 per cent of Duma deputies, reflecting the extent of unease in the Russian leadership.[29] It was perhaps in response to this sentiment that Russian Foreign Minister Sergei Ivanov insisted that the US forces in Central Asia will have to leave once their task of defeating terrorism was accomplished.[30]

Washington's response to the simmering anxiety in Moscow has been to downplay the long-term implications of its commitment to Central Asia in order to preserve the international coalition in the 'war on terror'. While on his third visit to Central Asia in January 2001, the US commander of the military operation in Afghanistan, General Tommy Franks, told journalists that Washington had no long-term plans to station troops or to 'build a permanent military base' in Central Asia.[31] He denied suggestions that the United States had signed a secret agreement with Tashkent to lease an Uzbek military base for twenty-five years, insisting that there was 'no competition whatsoever between Russia and the United States for spheres of influence' in Central Asia.[32]

Yet these assurances were not sufficient to alleviate Russian concerns. Writing in the conservative *Svobodnaya Mysl'*, Andranik Migranian lamented the deployment of US troops in Central Asia as the latest phase in Russia's 'withdrawal from the world'.[33] Another author in the same issue was more indignant, though fatalistic, about the new geostrategic shape of the region:

> Despite repeated statements by Washington that American military presence in Central Asia will be limited to anti-terrorist operations in Afghanistan, it seems clear that the United States will stay [in this region] for a long time – there is no time frame for their departure ... Uzbekistan will remain America's main strategic partner in Central Asia.[34]

President Karimov gave every indication that this assessment was accurate and that the new relationship with the United States was irreversible. Dismissing calls for a US withdrawal timeframe, he told his Central Asian counterparts in October 2002: 'Americans should not leave our region until peace and stability is established throughout Central Asia ... they should stay as long as needed.'[35]

Russian leaders have been visibly angered by such bold statements by Uzbek leaders. Boris Pastuthov, chairman of the Duma Central Asian Affairs Committee, expressed this widely felt displeasure when he warned Uzbekistan 'not to overstep the line'.[36] The Russian leadership interpreted the tense Russo–Uzbek relations against the background of US involvement in the region as an indication of a new challenge to Russia's position in Central Asia. This assessment seemed to be justified. The gradual deterioration of relations with Tajikistan, Russia's firmest regional ally and home to the Russian 201 motorised rifle division, was seen as proof of Russia's weakening authority. According to the deputy chairman of the Duma's committee on the CIS: 'Russian–Tajik relations have worsened sharply due to the closeness between Washington and Dushanbe. The United States behaviour in the region is aggressive, and Russia will not be able to remain inactive for much longer.'[37]

Moscow's move to establish an anti-terrorism rapid reaction force in Kant, Kyrgyzstan, in December 2002 was widely seen as a desperate measure to reverse its declining fortunes. The landing of Russian planes at Kant airbase was officially presented as an anti-terrorist initiative under the auspices of the CIS Collective Security Treaty.[38] But many observers were sceptical of Russia's intentions in locating its troops some twenty miles from the American base in Manas, exactly a year after the American-led operation toppled the Taliban. It was not surprising, therefore, that this move was greeted with cynicism in Central Asia. The Kazakhstan-based weekly *Kontinent* pointedly asked what prompted Moscow to take this decision, implying that fighting terrorism was not the real objective.[39] A later issue of the paper put it more bluntly: Russia's decision to establish the anti-terrorism rapid reaction force in Kant was designed to counter the pervasive 'American hegemony' in Central Asia.[40] That was precisely how the Uzbek president described the situation and warned that the move could result in a 'military rivalry' between the United States and Russia, with destabilising consequences for the region.[41]

Many Russian analysts have found the new challenge to Moscow's influence in Central Asia very disappointing, especially since President Vladimir Putin had tried to reverse the decline of Russia's role in the region.[42] Moscow had tried to appear open to the concerns of the Central Asian leaders. In a high-level visit by President Putin and his foreign minister, Sergei Ivanov, to Tashkent in May 2000, for example, Russian leaders promised to support Uzbekistan against threats emanating from Afghanistan.[43] But Putin's efforts to regain influence in the region have lost their force in the post-September 11 landscape of Central Asia. What has been even more disheartening for many Russian leaders and commentators, who saw Russia playing a significant role in Central Asia, is the aura of irreversibility surrounding the present geostrategic line-up.

Conclusion

On the eve of President Karimov's trip to Washington in March 2002, his press secretary Sadyk Safarov told Itar-Tass 'we have a common foe … an international terrorist network'.[44] This was a consistent line of argument that the Uzbek government had tried to push before and after September 11. The attacks on the New York Twin Towers and the Pentagon gave substance to this claim. The consequent anti-terrorist coalition brought Uzbekistan and the United States unprecedentedly close, with long-term implications. A year after the launch of the anti-terrorist campaign Elizabeth Jones, assistant secretary for European and Eurasian affairs in the State Department, was quoted as saying: 'America will not forget who supported us [in the war on terror]. When this conflict is over we are not going to forget Central Asia.'[45] She repeated this promise in Washington: 'When the Afghan conflict is over we will not leave Central Asia. We have long-term plans and interests in this region.'[46] This was precisely what the Uzbek leadership wished to hear. From the very start, Tashkent saw the 'war on terror' as an opportunity to win favour with the United States and consolidate bilateral relations. This overarching objective was significantly advanced in the course of the war in Afghanistan and the subsequent war in Iraq. Uzbekistan was recognised by Washington as a reliable partner against Islamic terrorism and, more importantly, as a leading power in Central Asia.

This partnership is primarily based on a shared fear of Islamic militancy, in the form of al-Qaeda and the IMU. The implications of this partnership are far-reaching. First, it has seriously affected the regional geostrategic dynamics in a direct affront to Moscow's self-designated role as the guarantor of regional security, and given a boost to Tashkent's aspirations for a more dominant role in Central

Asia. This radical shift in the regional balance of power has been unsettling for Moscow. For its part, Washington has tried to cushion the blow by insisting that (1) it does not wish to replace Russia in that region, and (2) its military operations will benefit Russia and regional security in the long run because Islamic terrorism poses an indiscriminate threat to all. The latter argument has been accepted by President Putin and his government, even if many in the Russian leadership remain highly sceptical. The removal of the Taliban from power was expected to deprive radical Islamic groups in the CIS from training facilities and this seemed to be sufficient reason for supporting the American campaign in the 'war on terror'.

Second, as a consequence of the new geostrategic reality in Central Asia, the Uzbek leadership feels liberated from its difficult relationship with Moscow. Even before the September 11 events, Uzbekistan repeatedly accused Russia of entertaining colonial ambitions and not recognising the sovereignty of the Central Asian states beyond formalities. This was a serious charge and counted for the tense relationship between Tashkent and Moscow. But at the same time, Tashkent was frustrated in its attempts to find another powerful ally to counter Russian influence. It was hoped by the Uzbek leadership that Uzbekistan's entry into the Shanghai Forum would offer it an opportunity to manoeuvre between China and Russia – even play them against each other. But the two great powers had very similar views on the region and left Tashkent little room for manoeuvre. Uzbek leadership was effectively caught between a rock and a hard place until September 11. The deployment of US troops to Central Asia and the rapidly developing security relations between the remaining superpower and this post-Soviet state threw a lifeline to the Uzbek leadership. The US–Uzbek partnership offered Tashkent an unprecedented opportunity to assert itself in the region and in relation to Russia, and this was done under the cover of fighting a common enemy. The 'war on terror' was the pretext for a major realignment in Central Asia.

Third, the benefits of the US–Uzbek partnership were not confined to Tashkent's regional ambitions. The Uzbek leadership gained domestically from its newly found international status. It felt vindicated in its response to the 'Islamic threat' and justified in pursuing its authoritarian practices. The much celebrated 'democratic reforms' in the US lexicon in relation to Central Asia, as will be explored in Chapter 6, were the first casualty of the security partnership. But the consolidation of the Uzbek authoritarian regime in its war on Islamic militancy could not be allowed to degrade its Islamic credentials. Just as the US administration systematically denied the 'war on terror' was a war on Islam, Uzbek authorities insisted that their campaign was consistent with Islam and their heritage. They even turned to the state-controlled Islamic clergy for its blessing, which was duly forthcoming. In an interview with *Rossiskaya Gazeta*, the Mufti of Uzbekistan endorsed the US-led war in Afghanistan and held the Taliban responsible for any civilian casualties.[47] This endorsement has been important for the credibility of the US operation. It has been even more important for the Uzbek regime and its orchestrated efforts to reinforce internal legitimacy. It is this domestic aspect of the US–Uzbek partnership that will be examined next.

Notes

1. RFE/RL, *NewsLine*, 18 September 2001.
2. Interfax, 25 September 2001.
3. Interfax, 19 September 2001.
4. Uzbek Radio, 1 October 2001.
5. Press Service of the President of the Republic of Uzbekistan, 26 September 2001.
6. Interfax, 17 October 2001.
7. Interfax, 4 November 2001.
8. The last large military operation, Anaconda, ended in March 2002. Romesh Ratnescar, 'Afghanistan: One Year Later', CNN *Inside Politics*, 10 October 2002, www.cnn.com/2002/ALLPOLITICS/10/10/timep.afghanistan.year.later.tm/.
9. Robert Kaiser, 'Uzbek–US Declaration Kept Secret', *Washington Post*, 1 July 2002.
10. UzReport.com, 13 March 2002.
11. Agence France Presse, 13 March 2002.
12. *Watanparvar*, 23 March 2002.
13. *Narodnoye Slovo*, 27 March 2002.
14. Allan Larsen, US undersecretary of state, told reporters: 'Uzbekistan holds a leading place in Central Asia', RIA Novosti, 14 December 2002.
15. See, for example, Pauline Jones Luong and Erika Weinthal, 'New Friends, New Fears in Central Asia', *Foreign Affairs*, vol. 81, no. 2, March–April 2002, pp. 61–70.
16. *Washington Post*, 30 December 2001.
17. Associated Press, 14 June 2002.

18. Agence France Presse, 8 December 2001.
19. RFE/RL, NewsLine, 17 April 2000.
20. Federal Information and News Dispatch, 14 April 2003.
21. RFE/RL, NewsLine, 11 November 2002.
22. Kontinent, 10 December 2002.
23. Bureau of European and Eurasian Affairs, 'US Government Assistance to and Cooperative Activities with Eurasia – FY 2002', released January 2003, www.state.gov/p/eur/rls/rpt/23630.htm.
24. Office of the Press Secretary, 'TDA Commits $3.5 million for Projects in Uzbekistan', 12 July 2002, www.state.gov/e/eb/rls/othr/11870. htm; Office of the Press Secretary, 'Coverage Opportunity: Delivery of US Military Hospital Equipment to Uzbekistan', 26 July 2002, www. state.gov/r/prs/ps/2002/12206.htm. Some observers estimate the total value of US aid to Uzbekistan in 2002 to be around US$500 million. See David Leigh, Nick Paton Walsh and Ewen MacAskill, 'Ambassador Accused after Criticising US', Guardian, 18 October 2003.
25. Richard Norton-Taylor, 'Export of Arms Criticised', Guardian, 27 February 2003.
26. RFE/RL, NewsLine, 27 September 2001.
27. Turkiston Press, 4 April 2002.
28. Nezavisimaya Gazeta, 9 October 2001.
29. RFE/RL, Newsline, 12 October 2001. This episode was discussed in Michael Rywkin, 'Central Asia in the Forefront of Attention', American Foreign Policy Interests 24, 2002, p. 40.
30. BBC News, 'Russia "Not Worried" by US Deployment', 13 February 2002, http://news.bbc.co.uk/2/hi/europe/1817458.stm.
31. RFE/RL, Newsline, 24 January 2002.
32. RFE/RL, Newsline, 25 January 2002.
33. Andranik Migranian, 'Konets Rossii?', Svobodnaya Mysl' 7, 2002, p. 7.
34. Stanislav Cherniavskii, 'Otstaivaia Natsional'nie Interesi: Politika Rossii v Tsentral'noi Asii i Zakavkaz'e', Svobodnaya Mysl' 7, 2002, p. 27.
35. Vasili Viktorov, Nezavisimaya Gazeta, 8 October 2002.
36. Inter Press Service, 24 October 2001. Some other Russian commentators reject Tashkent's close ties with the United States on different grounds. Sergei Prokurin of the Russian Academy argues that Tashkent's position is misguided and harmful to Uzbekistan's sovereignty. Uzbekistan's readiness to support every American action in the United Nations, he argues, has discredited the Uzbek leadership in the international community. The benefits of this close association with the United States are far from guaranteed. Sergei Prokurin, 'Mezhdunarodnye otnosheniya v postvestfal'skuyu epokhu', Svobodnaya Mysl' 5, 2003, pp. 64–71.
37. Viktoria Panfilova, Nezavisimaya Gazeta, 14 March 2003.
38. Viktoria Panfilova, Nezavisimaya Gazeta, 5 December 2002.
39. Sultan Akimbekov, 'Vozvraschenie Jedaia', Kontinent, 11–24 December 2002.
40. Konstantin Siroezhkin, 'Geopoliticheskii endshpiel', Kontinent, 15–21 January 2003.

41. RFE/RL, NewsLine, 12 December 2002.
42. For an analysis of Putin's achievements in Central Asia see, Roland Dannreuther, 'Can Russia Sustain Its Dominance in Central Asia?', Security Dialogue, vol. 32, no. 2, June 2001, pp. 245–8.
43. RFE/RL, NewsLine, 19 May 2000.
44. Itar-Tass News Agency, 5 March 2002.
45. Konstantin Siroezhkin, 'God posle tragedii', Kontinent, 18 September–1 October 2002.
46. Guardian, 11 March 2003.
47. Vladimir Berezovskiy, Rossiskaya Gazeta, 16 November 2001.

6

Human Rights and Democracy

On 17 October 2002 the British ambassador to Uzbekistan, Craig Murray, delivered a blistering attack on the authoritarian rule of the Uzbek government. Delivering the inaugural address on launching the Freedom House office in Tashkent, he declared:

> Uzbekistan is not a functioning democracy, nor does it appear to be moving in the direction of democracy. The major political parties are banned; parliament is not subject to democratic election and checks and balances on the authority of the executive are lacking....There is worse: we believe there to be between 7,000 and 10,000 people in detention whom we would consider as political and/or religious prisoners. In many cases they have been falsely convicted of crimes with which there appears to be no credible evidence they had any connection.[1]

This was a very controversial speech, which resulted in a diplomatic furore and forced the British ambassador to suspend his duties while recovering from stress caused by the backlash from the UK Foreign Office and the White House.[2]

The Uzbek government has been trying systematically to counter this dire assessment. Uzbekistan's involvement in the 'war on terror' and its close association with the United States raised expectations about prospects of political reform and improvements in the human rights record of this Central Asian republic. Carefully targeted signals from Tashkent seemed to give credence to this expectation. President Karimov's initiative to include political reforms in the text of the Strategic Partnership document was welcomed by many observers as a positive sign. At the very least, it was a clear indication that the Uzbek leadership was aware of the importance of this issue in the United States and more generally for Western public opinion, and its potential for harming the newly developed bilateral relations. Tashkent's sensitivity to this issue may be gauged by noting well-timed public announcements about the release of prisoners, abolition of media censorship and lifting of restrictions on public associations, often corresponding with official visits.

Yet these stage-managed steps towards political openness have failed to make a qualitative change in the authoritarian nature of Uzbek politics and its propensity to trample on human rights. The January 2002 referendum on extending the presidential term from five to seven years and creating a bicameral parliament offered a revealing, albeit rare, window on the political thinking and practice of President Karimov. Rejecting the familiar Western demand for transition to democracy, he stated that 'at a certain stage of historic change you need a strong will and a certain figure ... and you have to use some authoritarian methods at times'.[3] This statement was revealing, not only because it offered further proof of the Uzbek leadership's determination to reject the democratic model of government, in spite of public pronouncements to the contrary, but also because it showed that the leadership felt bold enough to state its position on the heels of its entry into the anti-terrorism coalition in Afghanistan. President Karimov's rebuff came against the backdrop of heightened international interest in Central Asia and betrayed a feeling of confidence that emanated from Tashkent's new partnership with the United States. Such episodes of frank disclosure, however, are not a common occurrence as the Uzbek leadership remains mindful of the potential harm its authoritarian image could inflict on its relations with the United States. As a result, researchers are confronted with the daunting task of exploring the true nature of the political philosophy of the leadership in a myriad of official declarations purporting to move Uzbekistan along a moderately angled trajectory to democratic rule and political openness.

Addressing the parliament after the controversial referendum in January 2000, President Karimov outlined the priorities of his government: to 'achieve a genuine multiparty atmosphere' to enable debate on opposing views; to step up the work of 'non-governmental organizations that are not opposed to the government'; to 'ensure the free expression of different ideas and diverse views' in the media; and to further develop human rights.[4] This chapter will focus on these broad areas that best illustrate the pace, or lack, of political reform in Uzbekistan. This chapter will illustrate that, in spite of consistent public declarations in Tashkent and commensurate expectations in the West, the US–Uzbek security partnership did not benefit the reform movement in a meaningful way.

Political Parties

The Uzbek regime has consistently worked towards the generation of an image of a multiparty political system. This image was thought to be an important feature of Uzbekistan's move away from Soviet-style one-party rule for domestic and external purposes. At the December 1999 parliamentary elections four parties gained representation in the Oliy Majlis: the People's Democratic Party (PDP), the Adolat Social-Democratic Party, the National Renaissance and Fidokorlar (Self-sacrificers). But beyond this multiparty façade, Uzbek politics was as authoritarian as its Soviet predecessor. None of these parties behaved in a fashion that could be interpreted as autonomous of the ruling regime. Instead they derived legitimacy from their commitment to President Karimov and his rule. They competed with each other not over divergent platforms or policy agenda, but over the extent of their loyalty to one man. In this respect, despite all appearances, politics in post-Soviet Uzbekistan had regressed from a system of one-party rule to a system of one-man rule.

It looks very unlikely that the political landscape will change significantly to bring about President Karimov's promise of a 'genuine multiparty system' in the wake of Uzbekistan's parliamentary elections of December 2004. This must be disappointing for dissidents. The new security realignment with the United States in the post-September 11 era was seen by some dissidents in Uzbekistan as offering a window of opportunity. They sought to take advantage of the rare international spotlight on their country to reclaim a position in the political system. But this effort was effectively suppressed even before its launch. On 25 May 2002 activists from the banned opposition party Erk were planning to gather in Tashkent to use the unprecedented international media interest in Uzbekistan as a cover to lobby for Erk's registration. That morning, police detained Atonazar Arifov, the party's first secretary, and prevented him from attending the meeting.[5] The meeting was consequently cancelled.

The failed attempt to regain legal status for Erk reinforced the impression that the ruling regime, far from being interested in promoting a multiparty system, cannot tolerate opposition. President Karimov has ensured that Erk remains an ineffective and illegal organisation by subjecting its exiled leader to criminal charges, widely regarded by Western observers as fabricated. Muhammad Solih, founder of Erk, was judged in absentia for his alleged involvement in the February 1999 bombing in Tashkent and found guilty. He was sentenced to death.[6] This was a further blow to Erk and its chances of regaining credibility in Uzbekistan. But it might be argued that the authorities' treatment of Erk and its supporters was relatively mild in comparison with the treatment of Islamic dissidents. It might also be argued that international media attention in the post-September 11 era prevented a harsher response to Erk activists attending the May 2002 meeting.

A recent development gave some credence to the above point of view. On 14 June 2003 Erk finally held its first congress in ten years in Tashkent, about a month after Birlik held a similar meeting. This was an unprecedented development and Erk leaders were quietly optimistic about their chances of gaining legal status as a political party and participating in the December 2004 parliamentary elections.[7] Remarkably none of the thirty delegates to the congress was arrested. This 'success', as Muhammad Solih called it, has excited observers about the possibilities of greater openness in Uzbek politics. This, and other occasional evidence, has led the US administration to present an optimistic appraisal of Uzbekistan's movement towards political openness and respect for human rights. According to a congressional testimony by Secretary of State Colin Powell, Uzbekistan is making 'substantial and continuing progress' in meeting its human rights and democracy commitments proclaimed in the US–Uzbek Joint Declaration.[8] This assessment was critical for the congressional release of $45 million extra funds to Uzbekistan.

Veteran analysts such as Bruce Pannier of Radio Liberty, however, are more circumspect in their assessment and view this episode as 'a small sign of encouragement'.[9] It is difficult not to draw a link between this development and Uzbekistan's new international status. Atonazar Arifov attributed this apparent turn in Erk's fortunes to the international media scrutiny of Uzbek affairs.[10] There may be some truth in this assertion. But this possible link has not had any impact on the authorities' approach to Islamic groups. The relatively restrained handling of Erk activists could be a reflection of the leadership's sense of invulnerability to secular dissidents.

The authorities' treatment of those suspected of affiliation with Islamic groups is significantly harsher. The Islamic Movement of Uzbekistan and Hizb ut-Tahrir are branded terrorist; the fact that the latter explicitly rejects political violence and maintains a legal operation in Europe has made no impression on Tashkent. Consequently, anyone suspected of harbouring political Islamic aspirations is subjected to judicial prosecution and extrajudicial physical and psychological abuse. The death of two suspected Hizb ut-Tahrir prisoners in August 2002 came as a shock to those who expected a modification of state behaviour in relation to political dissent and respect for human rights. In a document released by the America-based Human Rights Watch, Elizabeth Andersen, executive director of the Europe and Central Asia Division, argued that Tashkent's promises of political reform and progress in its human rights records 'were mere window-dressing, intended to hide Uzbekistan's persistent problem and placate international critics.'[11]

The Uzbek authorities' persistent campaign against Islamic activists has continued unabated into 2003. The rejection of Islamic dissidents as 'Wahhabi' and terrorist is illustrative of two important facts: (1) Tashkent intends to present its repressive policies as part of the international 'war on terror', and (2) it hopes to denigrate the Islamic opposition as criminals, linked to a foreign source which has nothing to do with national culture and traditions. Tashkent's success in achieving this double objective is difficult to assess, especially at the street level. But the official clergy appears to endorse the portrayal of Islamists as alien to Uzbek Islam. In a revealing 1999 case, Mufti Abdurashid Qori Bahromov dismissed female students' hijab as a 'foreign' practice, 'anathema to the form

of Islam embraced by the majority of the population'.[12] This charge
has been repeatedly used against Hizb ut-Tahrir followers for acting
against Uzbek traditions, whether purposefully or by default. In a
somewhat reconciliatory manner, the Uzbek minister of the interior,
Zohirjon Almatov, referred to Hizb ut-Tahrir supporters as simply
'deceived' into supporting an anti-Uzbek organisation.[13] A similar
point was made by Shoazim Munavvarov, chairman of the Committee
for Religious Affairs, in an interview with Uzbekistan's daily *Pravda
Vostoka*: some youth find it difficult to reject foreign religious ideas
and the financial incentives offered by Hizb ut-Tahrir.[14] In essence the
message that various government officials and the Islamic establishment have been systematically conveying is that Islamic opposition
to the Uzbek regime has no justification in authentic Islam or
national traditions and is therefore illegitimate. This is a powerful
line of argument with conspicuous reference to Uzbek nationalism,
a potent force that has the potential to carry the largely apolitical
citizens of Uzbekistan.

According to Uzbek authorities, a line could be drawn between
being duped into believing in an alien ideology in contradiction
with national traditions and engaging in terrorist acts. But this is
a very thin line. An Uzbek state television programme portrayed
a logical, even natural, link between women in hijab and suicide
bombers. Referring to the Nord-Ost hostage-taking by Chechen
militants, among them women in full black attire, which ended in
the death of 200 people, the presenter argued:

> there are some women, unfortunately, among us, who come from a
> foreign country, the Middle East or the South ... dressed in black, they
> bring their ideas to our country. Yesterday we saw it in Moscow: first
> they dress in black, then arm our women with pistols, then tie explosives
> on them ... and order them to kill themselves, to cause damage to their
> own people.[15]

This bleak assessment was endorsed by the interior minister and chair
of a neighbourhood women's committee on the same programme.

The only dissenting voice to this logic has been raised by
Muhammad Sadyk, a former mufti who returned to Uzbekistan in
2000 after seven years of self-exile.[16] While not challenging the charge
that Islamists are misled into 'un-Uzbek' and un-Islamic behaviour,
he has argued that the best way to deal with them would be to

provide re-education. That Muhammad Sadyk's implicit criticism of the heavy-handed approach to practising Muslims did not provoke an attack on the former mufti may be seen as a tangible benefit of the continued international interest in Uzbekistan.

The Uzbek regime claims monopoly over Islam and the nation. It seeks to define what makes the genuine Muslim Uzbek. The regime cannot accommodate political pluralism because it fears that by withdrawing control its carefully constructed version of Islamic authority and national heritage would become open to challenge by contending views. This could have highly detrimental repercussions for its hold on power. Contrary to grand declarations by officials, the Uzbek regime has shown no indication of opening the public space to competing interests and perspectives. The complete lack of interest in such a process is conspicuously visible in Tashkent's handling of Hizb ut-Tahrir – but is not confined to that party. The Uzbek regime has shown contempt for independent social and human rights organisations which are deemed to challenge its authority.

Human Rights and NGOs

The Soviet collapse and subsequent Western interest in supporting civil society in the post-Soviet space have contributed to the emergence of a plethora of non-governmental organisations. According to a rough estimate by M. Holt Ruffin and Daniel Waugh, Uzbekistan's NGOs in 1999 numbered around seventy.[17] These ranged from women's associations to educational and exchange agencies. Financial grants from international organisations, Western governments and philanthropic foundations, such as the Soros Foundation, have encouraged the spread of NGOs in Uzbekistan. It is, however, important to note that this apparent freedom of association does not extend to public initiatives that have the potential to question the political legitimacy of the ruling regime. Associations concerned with the protection of human rights have particularly found it difficult to gain registration though the Ministry of Justice.

Tashkent's treatment of two human rights organisations, the Human Rights Society of Uzbekistan (HRSU) and the Independent Organisation for Human Rights in Uzbekistan (IOHRU), bear testimony to this claim. In March 2002, the IOHRU achieved formal registration as a public organisation, some ten years after its first application.[18] This was hailed by the US administration as a significant step, but human rights conditions in Uzbekistan have not enjoyed a parallel improvement to justify this positive assessment.

In September 2002, Yoldash Rasulev, chairman and founding member of the HRSU, was sentenced to seven years in jail on charges of conspiracy to overthrow the constitutional order in Uzbekistan. According to witnesses, the only evidence presented at his trial was that Rasulev 'prayed five times a day and had listened to tapes on Islam ... and helped people persecuted for their religious beliefs and affiliations'.[19] Rasulev received a presidential pardon in January 2003, but systematic persecution of human rights activists persists. Other members of the HRSU and the IOHRU have suffered similarly harsh treatment by the authorities. Human Rights Watch has catalogued various forms of pressure on these organisations and their members in its *World Report* 2003.[20] Reported cases of prosecution highlight the political nature of charges against NGO activists and reveal the Uzbek judiciary's lack of independence from the ruling regime.

Uzbek human rights NGOs, however, appear to have received a welcome boost from international agencies. The opening of a Freedom House office in Tashkent in October 2002 was a significant milestone. Funded by the State Department and US Agency for International Development, the Freedom House initiative in Central Asia aims to enhance indigenous human rights groups' effectiveness in their campaigns. The opening of the Namangan office of Freedom House in June 2003 was a further reminder of that organisation's persistent interest in improving human rights conditions in Uzbekistan. To its credit Freedom House has had some success in consolidating the efforts of Uzbek human rights groups. Plans for the launch of the Working Group for Public Monitoring of Uzbek Legislation Regulating the Activity of Nongovernmental and Noncommercial Organizations, under the aegis of Freedom House, to deal with 'repressive and discriminatory' laws, hint at a long-term strategy.[21] This point was illustrated in October 2003 when Freedom House provided the venue for the fourth congress of the HRSU, which was also sponsored by the British Embassy and the OSCE Center.[22]

The Freedom House initiative in Uzbekistan enjoys the support of the US State Department as US officials appreciate the public-relations importance of promoting political openness and civil society. According to Assistant Secretary of State Elizabeth Jones, the new foreign policy illustrates the 'US commitment to engagement and dialogue'. Jones concluded her presentation at the University of Montana, Missoula, by rejecting the pre-September 11 policy:

> There are those who would argue that some of these countries in the region – because of their human rights or corruption records – deserve to be sanctioned or that we should turn our back on them until they learn to behave. I do not deny that there are problems, but legislatively imposed sanctions are not the answer. Sanctions do not ensure that countries will fall in line.[23]

It remains to be seen to what extent this new policy of engagement will promote respect for human rights, rule of law and public accountability in Uzbekistan.

International pressure to promote the human rights record in Uzbekistan has had limited effect. The Uzbek regime has successfully managed to avoid making fundamental changes in its conduct while offering minimal concessions to placate Western concerns. The 2003 annual conference of the European Bank for Reconstruction and Development (EBRD) offered a glimpse into the Uzbek leadership's 'balancing act'. In late 2002 arrangements for the EBRD's scheduled meeting for May 2003 came under question following a UN report on widespread torture and violation of human rights in Uzbek prisons (to be discussed below). Jean Lemierre, head of EBRD, responded to this report by stating that the 'EBRD doesn't rule out the possibility of a change of venue ... we have serious concerns about Uzbekistan'.[24] Faced with this potentially humiliating scenario, the Uzbek leadership tried to allay European concerns. Meeting with EU foreign ministers in January 2003, the Uzbek foreign minster, Abdulaziz Kamilov, admitted 'we do not meet all international (human rights) standards' – a transparent strategy to disarm his critics. Kamilov promised progress on that front and, as per earlier occasions in US–Uzbek meetings, signed a joint statement to reiterate 'the vital necessity of respect for human rights and fundamental freedoms in the fight against terrorism'.[25]

In the end, the EBRD proceeded with its annual meeting in May 2003 at the planned venue. It did, however, offer an opportunity to Uzbek human rights organisations to address an international audience and present their grievances against the systematic abuse of power in Uzbekistan. This was hailed by many observers as a significant achievement. President Islam Karimov was also scheduled to address the meeting, and there was an air of expectation among foreign reporters that he would use this opportunity to condemn openly and unequivocally human rights violations and torture.[26] He did not. Instead President Karimov used the occasion to claim success in ensuring media freedom, the rule of law, political accountability and, poignantly, hailing the US–Uzbek partnership against Islamic terrorism.[27] This was a disappointing, but not surprising, outcome for Uzbek human rights activists.[28]

Political Prisoners and Torture

Uzbekistan has been criticised by local human rights groups and international agencies for prosecuting its citizens for their religious and political beliefs. The Human Rights Watch coordinator in Tashkent put the number of political prisoners at between 7,000 and 10,000.[29] Other sources, including the US State Department, agree that this may be a conservative estimate. A great majority of these prisoners have been held on suspicion of links with Islamic groups such as the IMU and Hizb ut-Tahrir. There were even reports that men with beards, which is generally seen as a sign of religious piety in Muslim societies, were routinely detained and questioned by security forces because of assumed links with Islamic extremism.[30] This pattern of discrimination and harassment continues in the prison system. According to a November 2003 report issued by Keston News Services, prisoners were transferred to punishment cells for observing fast in the month of Ramadan. Others were asked to sign declarations denouncing political Islamism and reject public observance of Islamic rituals.[31] These claims are vehemently rejected by Uzbek authorities.

Reports of torture in Uzbek prisons have caused a stir in the international human rights community and put significant pressure on the Uzbek regime. Such claims led to the first UN Report on Torture in Uzbekistan – a damning document which discredited Uzbek authorities' attempts to whitewash the abysmal condition of human rights for prisoners of conscience. In December 2002, Theo van Boven, Professor of International Law at Maastricht University in the Netherlands, investigated charges of torture in Uzbekistan. He was impeded in his mission by lack of cooperation from local authorities: 'I have to say that I could not carry out my visit to Jaslyk in a satisfactory and comprehensive manner.' Jaslyk, which houses political prisoners, has a reputation for harsh conditions. Navoi'i and Karshi prisons were also off-limits due to bad weather. He also complained of the limited time allotted to his visits to other prison facilities.[32]

Professor van Boven argued, nonetheless, that the evidence on torture was compelling and could not be dismissed out of hand: 'I do not think that the fact that I saw some institutions in a limited way and some others I could not visit ... undermine the credibility and the well-founded nature of the findings which I'm going to present.'[33] Boven told reporters in Tashkent: 'torture as far as I can see ... is not just incidental but systemic in nature'.[34] A formal report of his findings was submitted to the 59th session of the UN Commission on Human Rights, held in Geneva (17 March–25 April 2003), prompting an ·official rebuke from Uzbek authorities.[35] The aforementioned EBRD annual meeting in Tashkent was held shortly after the release of this report and caused disappointment for many human rights campaigners.

According to Amnesty International, torture in pre-trial cases is often used to extract confession of guilt. In one such reported case, a man confessed to being a member of the IMU and was sentenced to death by the court in November 2002. This ruling was upheld by the appeals court in January 2003, even after the representing lawyer and Amnesty International requested an independent inquiry into torture allegations.[36] Such incidents have led many observers to question the independence of the judiciary, a critical issue that was highlighted in the UN Report on Torture in Uzbekistan.

Another aspect of the human rights record in Uzbekistan is the forcible commitment of human rights activists to psychiatric treatment. One prominent case was Elena Urlaeva, a leading member of the HRSU, who was committed for psychiatric treatment on two occasions in 2001 and 2002, each time after she took part in protest rallies.[37] This and similar cases led Holly Cartner of Human Rights

Watch to speak of a 'throwback to the ugliest Soviet repression against dissident movements of the 1970s'.[38] The revival of this crude repressive measure could not but cause indignation among international human rights organisations and give them more impetus.

The record of the International Committee of the Red Cross (ICRC) in this regard is remarkable. After years of lobbying, the ICRC finally gained permission from Tashkent to inspect Uzbekistan's prison system in January 2001.[39] The ICRC was given permission to visit prisons and detention centres, and to conduct confidential interviews with inmates. But the ICRC team soon discovered that there is a wide gap between formal treaties on human rights and implementation of international agreements on the ground.[40] Faced with uncooperative local officials who denied ICRC access to some prisons or created an atmosphere in which it was impossible for the inspection team to conduct confidential interviews with detainees, the ICRC announced its withdrawal from Uzbekistan in April 2002, ironically only a few weeks after the government reconfirmed its commitment to protecting human rights and democratic institutions in the Uzbek–US Declaration on Strategic Partnership (March 2002). The ICRC's withdrawal from Uzbekistan was greeted with dismay by various international agencies,[41] among them the EBRD, which raised the issue with the Uzbek foreign minister, Kamilov, in January 2003.[42] That the ICRC was readmitted to Uzbekistan in the same month may have been related to mounting international pressure. According to the ICRC in June 2003, 'difficulties preventing the ICRC from starting credible visits ... have been to a great extent overcome ... The ICRC has carried out twelve visits to nine places of detention under the ministry of interior since January 2003.'[43] A condition for this access is that the ICRC should refrain from making public statements about its findings in Uzbekistan.

As a result of growing international pressure and the proliferation of domestic human rights activism, some small steps appear to have been taken at least to open up Uzbekistan's treatment of political prisoners and detainees to international scrutiny. There has already been at least one report of some improvement in the condition of prisoners as a result of international attention.[44] The presidential amnesty in December 2002 to over 900 prisoners was welcomed as a positive gesture by the US administration. It is far from certain, however, that these improvements are irreversible. US Ambassador John Herbst's ominous assessment in April 2003 that, so far as human rights and independent journalism were concerned, 'much of the old [Soviet] system remained in place', still holds.[45] This is in spite of cosmetic reforms that have given the US State Department cause for celebration.

Freedom of Expression

Media censorship in Uzbekistan officially ended in mid-2002, completing a two-step process. In May the head of Uzbekistan's agency for protecting state secrets was removed and the State Press Committee was divested of its power to cut or demand changes in press articles.[46] This was widely interpreted by observers in the West as a significant step away from media censorship. Shortly after, the State Press Committee was transformed into the Uzbek Press and Information Agency by presidential decree (July 2002). The new agency was categorically forbidden 'to carry out censorship, editing, bans and other forms of illegal interference in the work of the media'.[47] A new law on the freedom of information was subsequently adopted, purporting to guarantee and safeguard 'the right of everyone to seek, receive, research, disseminate, use and store information'. Article Eight of this law further declares 'in the republic of Uzbekistan censorship and monopolization of information are prohibited'.[48]

While these measures seemed significant, and have often been cited by the US administration as evidence of progress, it would be naive to take them as a turning point. Uzbek journalists, even the brave few who have tried to test their new freedoms, remain fully aware of the limitations of such legal and administrative announcements and appear unable or reluctant to challenge government officials. Self-censorship by Uzbek journalists to avoid job insecurity or loss of liberty appears to remain an effective impediment to media freedom. Subsequent to the May 2002 shake-up, a delegation from the New York-based Committee to Protect Journalists condemned Uzbekistan as the only country in Europe and Central Asia that imprisoned its journalists 'for carrying out their professional duties'.[49] The committee concluded that the formal abolition of censorship did not fundamentally improve the working conditions of journalists.[50]

It has been argued by some human rights groups that the official lifting of pre-publication censorship made editors even more responsible for the material they published. According to the representative of Human Rights Watch in Uzbekistan:

> it's clear that the government still has a very strict control over the content of the media. After censorship – that was pre-publication censorship – all the heads of the media organisations were called to Tashkent.... They were told that they were now responsible to ensure that the contents of their publications remain as they were before. If articles were being published which weren't in line with the government requirements, the editors would have to answer for that. Similar meetings were held in all the regions of Uzbekistan.[51]

Consequently, self-censorship gained greater significance in the eyes of the Uzbek regime and measures were taken to encourage it. A systematic campaign of harassment and persecution appears to have been unleashed in early 2003 to remind journalists of the ever-present perils of filing reports critical of the ruling regime and its office holders. These media-related incidents gave the lie to claims of freedom of expression in Uzbekistan. On 20 February 2003, merely two weeks after the publication of the Law 'On the Principles and Guarantees of the Freedom of Information', Tokhtomurad Toshev, editor of the *Adolat* weekly, was arrested in his office. No formal charges were laid against him.[52] Toshev's arrest came on the heels of the arrest and sentencing of another journalist charged with inciting religious dissent and violence in his articles.[53] The pattern of official harassment of journalists continued with the arrest of Ergash Bobozhonov on charges of threatening to murder and disclosure of state secrets. The first charge related to a 1994 incident when Bobozhonov allegedly threatened to run someone over with a car; the second charge emanated from a series of articles he published in *Respublika*, across the border in Kyrgyzstan.[54]

In March 2003 the editor of *Hurriyat* newspaper, Amirkul Karimov, was summoned to the presidential administration office and asked to resign from his post. He was also dismissed as head of the

National Press Centre. Amirkul Karimov was the second editor of *Hurriyat*, appointed to the job after his predecessor was dismissed in 1996. No official reason was given for Karimov's dismissal, but it was seen among Uzbek human rights activists as a reaction to the paper's publication of a number of probing articles into corruption among office holders.[55] Given the salient pattern of reprimands and dismissals directed at journalists investigating social malaise, it is difficult to dismiss the above explanation for Karimov's removal from *Hurriyat*'s editorship. The incident was specially revealing because *Hurriyat* is hailed as the only independent newspaper – it is not tied to any political party or government agency. But the presidential office reserves the right to appoint and dismiss its editor, a transparent impediment to its freedom.

It was against this background of 'hidden censorship' that a frustrated Tashkent resident called an Uzbek radio talk-back programme to complain of pervasive corruption in the country and transparent obstacles preventing the media from scrutinising them. He was promptly taken off the air for 'technical reasons' and the subject was changed.[56] This would have been an insignificant episode, were it not a vivid reminder of the effectiveness of self-censorship.

The campaign of harassment against independent journalists is, of course, not confined to locals. Foreign correspondents also suffer various degree of harassment, ranging from being scolded by the presidential press secretary for asking difficult questions, to physical attacks by thugs in the street for reporting protest rallies. Two reporters from Radio Free Europe/Radio Liberty and the Voice of America were beaten in full view of Tashkent police on 6 March 2003. They were interviewing women demonstrating in support of their husbands and other male relatives jailed for their alleged involvement with Hizb ut-Tahrir.[57]

The Uzbek regime's harsh treatment of local and foreign journalists and the campaign of harassment and intimidation designed to enforce media self-censorship have clearly undermined the credibility of official claims regarding the abolition of censorship. Numerous reports on the maltreatment of journalists and editors forced the State Department spokesperson Richard Boucher to remind the government of Uzbekistan that 'harassment of journalists is a serious violation of basic democratic principles'.[58]

Conclusion

There are serious concerns among some observers and analysts that
the security partnership between the United States and Uzbekistan
will bolster authoritarianism in the latter. Pauline Jones Luong and
Erika Weinthal warned that Uzbek and Tajik leaders were likely to use
the new strategic line-up to step up their 'crackdowns on political
opposition in general and on Islamists in particular. They will also
expect Washington to be less critical of any human rights violations
they commit along the way.'[59] This pertinent assessment explains
the awkward nature of US–Uzbek relations. The record of Tashkent's
behaviour in the period since September 11 and the formation of
the anti-terror coalition gives credence to the above assessment. The
Uzbek regime has done little of substance to address democratic
aspirations. It remains fully committed to maintaining complete
control over the political processes, institutions and discourse. It is
suspicious of grassroots organisations with a seemingly threatening political agenda. That is the reason independent human rights
groups are considered a threat: they have the potential to expose
the misconduct of office holders and undermine the legitimacy of
the regime.

Uzbekistan's legal and electoral systems have remained unreformed
in the post-September 11 period. A genuine multiparty system remains
out of bounds and media freedom is a fictitious claim. These were
the points of reference for the US–Uzbek Strategic Partnership of
March 2002. The US administration now finds itself in a position
where it has to speak in two tongues on Uzbekistan. On the one
hand, the Bush administration is pleased with the security measures
in Central Asia and Uzbekistan's role in fighting terrorism. It also
views positively public statements issued in Tashkent regarding
President Karimov's commitment to political and economic reforms.
These declarations are seen as promising progress in the right
direction. But the administration, specifically the State Department,
which has traditionally been a force for the promotion of political
openness in the former Soviet states, cannot but be disappointed by
the almost intangible results of reforms in Uzbekistan. The discour-
aged expression of dismay in March 2003 by the State Department
spokesperson regarding continued restrictions on media freedom

revealed a sense of frustration, albeit unspoken, with the lack of progress in Uzbekistan. But this frustration has not been enough to dissuade the Uzbek leadership from pursuing the consolidation of the status quo.

Political reform has not yet reached Uzbekistan. Instead the regime has used the cover of the 'war on terror' and its newly acquired role in the US-led coalition to continue its policy of eliminating political dissent. There is a realisation in Tashkent that Washington is no longer making its geostrategic interests hostage to the democratisation agenda, and this has offered Uzbek leaders a degree of freedom in their conduct. The relentless crackdown on suspected supporters of Hizb ut-Tahrir and the IMU suggests that (1) the regime still feels vulnerable to the challenge of Islamism and (2) it feels assured of Washington's support in suppressing alleged Islamists. The fear of growing Islamism may be justified, but Tashkent's heavy-handed approach is likely to make matters worse. In an interview with the Russian daily *Nezavisimaya Gazeta*, Azizulla Gaziev, an expert analyst with the International Crisis Group, argued that the Uzbek regime's policy of indiscriminate persecution was leading to greater social radicalisation. This process, said Gaziev, was undermining the inherently apolitical nature of Uzbeks.[60]

Notes

1. David Stern, 'British Envoy's Speech Reverberates in Uzbekistan', *EurasiaNet*, 14 January 2003, www.eurasianet.org/departments/rights/articles/eavo11403_pr.shtml.
2. Jonathan Ungoed-Thomas and Mark Franchetti, 'The British Ambassador Says His Hosts Are Boiling People To Death...', *Sunday Times*, 26 October 2003, p. 17.
3. RFE/RL, *Newsline*, 28 January 2002.
4. Uzbek Television first channel, 22 January 2000.
5. RFE/RL, *NewsLine*, 28 May 2002.
6. RFE/RL, *NewsLine*, 16 November 2000.
7. Bruce Pannier, 'Uzbek Opposition Meets Openly for First Time in 10 Years', RFE/RL, *Weekday Magazine*, 20 June 2003.
8. Human Rights Watch, *Uzbekistan: U.S. Rubber Stamps Human Rights*, 9 September 2002, http://hrw.org/press/2002/09/uzbeko909.htm.
9. Pannier, 'Uzbek Opposition Meets Openly for First Time in 10 Years'.
10. RFE/RL, *NewsLine*, 16 June 2003.

11. Human Rights Watch, *Uzbekistan: Two Brutal Deaths in Custody*, 10 August 2002, http://hrw.org/press/2002/08/uzbek081002.htm.

12. Human Rights Watch, *Uzbekistan Class Dismissed: Discriminatory Expulsions of Muslim Students*, October 1999, vol. 11, no. 12, www.hrw.org/reports/1999/uzbekistan/uzbek-02.htm.

13. Interview with Interior Ministry, Associated Press, 8 July 2002.

14. *Pravda Vostoka*, 1 November 2002, p. 3.

15. Uzbek Television first channel, 31 October 2002.

16. Uzbek Television first channel, 7 January 2000.

17. M. Holt Ruffin and Daniel Waugh, eds, *Civil Society in Central Asia* (Seattle and London: Center for Civil Society International in association with University of Washington Press, 1999), pp. 295–310.

18. RFE/RL, *NewsLine*, 6 March 2002.

19. United Press International, 10 January 2003.

20. Human Rights Watch, *World Report* 2003.

21. RFE/RL, *NewsLine*, 2 May 2003.

22. REF/RL, *NewsLine*, 9 October 2003.

23. Federal Information and News Dispatch, 14 April 2003.

24. Agence France Presse, 17 December 2002.

25. Associated Press, 27 January 2003.

26. Agence France Presse, 2 May 2003.

27. Uzbek Television first channel, 4 May 2003.

28. Agence France Presse, 5 May 2003.

29. IRINnews Asia, 26 December 2002.

30. Not surprisingly, these charges are rejected by Uzbek authorities as baseless. According to Shoazim Munavvarov, chairman of the State Committee for Religious Affairs: 'in reality, all conditions have been created in Uzbekistan for freely performing all religious needs, including the five pillars of Islam. No one is persecuted for his faith, for growing a beard, for praying or wearing a scarf.' For the full interview, see *Pravda Vostoka*, 1 November 2002.

31. Igor Rotar, 'Prisoners Punished For Observing Ramadan', Keston News Service, 20 November 2002.

32. Josh Machleder, 'Despite Limited Access, UN Envoy Finds Torture throughout Uzbekistan', *EurasiaNet.Org*, 9 December 2002, www.eurasianet.org/departments/rights/articles/eav120902a_pr.shtml.

33. Ibid.

34. Agence France Presse, 17 December 2002.

35. See Appendix B for extracts of the UN Report. The complete Report may be found on this site: http://193.194.138.190/Huridocda/Huridoca.nsf/0/29d0f1eaf87cf3eac1256ce9005a0170/$FILE/G0310766.pdf. For the Uzbek government's rebuttal, see the official document dated 18 March 2003 presented by the Information Agency Jahon of the Ministry of Foreign Affairs of the Republic of Uzbekistan: 'Uzbekistan Underscores its Adherence to the Rule of Law', http://jahon.mfa.uz.

36. Associated Press, 28 January 2003.

37. Human Rights Watch, *World Report 2003: Uzbekistan*. Available at www.hrw. org/wr2k3/europe16.html.

38. 'Uzbekistan: Dissident in Psychiatric Detention Soviet-era Tactic Revived in Campaign against Human Rights Activists', *Uzbekistan Daily Digest*, 12 April 2001, www.eurasianet.org/resource/uzbekistan/hypermail/200104/0023.html.

39. 'Uzbek Delegation Discusses Human Rights Issues with EU', RFE/RL, *NewsLine*, 24 January 2001, www.rferl.org/newsline/2001/01/240101. asp.

40. Robert Kaiser, 'US Ties Inspire Uzbek Reform Promises', *Washington Post*, 1 July 2002.

41. Human Rights Watch, *World Report 2002: Uzbekistan*, www.hrw.org/wr2k2/europe22.html.

42. Associated Press, 27 January 2003.

43. Agence France Presse, 17 June 2003.

44. International journalists were invited to visit the Jaslyk colony in June 2003. Jaslyk is located in the inhospitable deserts of Karakalpak and is known among inmates as the 'place of no-return'. In December 1992 the UN Special Rapporteur was denied access to this colony. The subsequent visit by international journalists was intended to counter the highly critical UN report (see Appendix B). Associated Press (29 June 2003) recounts anecdotes from Uzbek prisoners: 'Ikromov [prisoner] said at least 20 prisoners had died since he arrived, four of them from his cell. Kulumbetov [prison supervisor] refused to give any figures on prisoners' deaths. Many prisoners said treatment had improved since last year's killings, which attracted a lot of attention from human rights groups and foreign news media. They said systematic beatings stopped and the basement cells where the killings allegedly happened were closed.'

45. Associated Press, 10 April 2003.

46. RFE/RL, *NewsLine*, 10 May 2002.

47. Uzbek National News Agency, 3 July 2002, www.uza.uz.

48. Law 'On the Principles and Guarantees of the Freedom of Information' was published in *Narodnoe Slovo*, 7 February 2003.

49. 'International Committee Calls on Uzbekistan to Stop Media Restriction', *Uzbekistan Daily Digest*, 21 June 2002, www.eurasianet.org/resource/uzbekistan/hypermail/news/0010.shtml.

50. 'Continued Absence of Media Freedom in Uzbekistan Criticized', *Uzbekistan Daily Digest*, 21 June 2002, www.eurasianet.org/resource/uzbekistan/hypermail/news/0007.shtml.

51. IRINnews Asia, 26 December 2002.

52. Associated Press, 21 February 2003.

53. Agence France Presse, 3 March 2003.

54. Associated Press, 22 February 2003.

55. Associated Press, 14 March 2003.

56. Uzbek Radio First Programme, Tashkent, 13 May 2003.

57. United Press International, 7 March 2003.

58. Agence France Presse, 3 March 2003.
59. Pauline Jones Luong and Erika Weinthal, 'New Friends, New Fears in Central Asia', *Foreign Affairs*, vol. 81, no. 2, March–April 2002, pp. 64–5.
60. *Nezavisimaya Gazeta*, 15 December 2001.

7

Prospects for Authoritarian Withdrawal

Uzbek authoritarianism is adaptive and self-generating. It has exhibited a remarkable ability to preserve itself while entering a new and more challenging international environment. Uzbekistan's involvement in the 'war on terror' and the much celebrated partnership treaty with the United States have brought this Central Asian state into closer contact with the United States and international organisations. Uzbekistan, as a member of the United Nations, is subject to UN-defined human rights expectations. With Washington's support, Uzbekistan has been exploring its future in line with IMF recommendations. It has already joined the European Bank for Reconstruction and Development. These memberships subject Uzbekistan to direct international pressure for political and economic reform. But the Uzbek regime has so far managed to avoid making substantial changes to its modus operandi. The regime continues its authoritarian practices of barring independent civil society initiatives from the political arena and systematically persecuting and prosecuting dissidents, routinely accusing them of harbouring Islamic fanatical views. At the same time, the Uzbek leadership makes conciliatory gestures and periodically confirms its intention to implement wide-ranging reforms. There is a salient disjuncture between Uzbekistan's declaratory and operational politics.

Interpretations of this gap vary. An increasingly influential group within the US academy and policymaking circles sees this as a natural aspect of transition to democracy. Uzbekistan cannot put its Soviet experience behind it overnight, so the argument runs; these things take time. Frederick Starr expressed this point most poignantly when he addressed the Sub-committee on Central Asia and South Caucasus of the US Senate Committee on Foreign Relations in December 2001. Explaining to US senators why the world should not expect miracles in Central Asia, Starr observed that 'ten years of independence is a very short time'. Referring to the US experience of building a constitutional democracy, by way of comparison, he continued: 'In 1786 [ten years after its Declaration of Independence] the US had no Supreme Court, slavery existed even in parts of the North, women were excluded from citizenship, and one of the models for the White House included a throne room.'[1] This comparison, however, suffers from an obvious flaw. The American experience was unique. The War of Independence and the formalisation of the constitutional democracy set a precedent for emancipatory movements worldwide. Even the celebrated French Revolution of 1789 and the legendary storming of the Bastille came on the heels of the American revolt against the *ancien régime* and the experiment with constructing a representative government. American revolutionaries had no role model, or foreign assistance, in this regard.

Uzbekistan's situation could not be further from this example. The Soviet experience, despite all its obvious limitations, put in place a comprehensive education system that made Central Asia very distinct from the rest of the Middle East. Uzbekistan boasts a literacy rate of 99 per cent with an impressive higher education entry record. This system brought to the highly educated Uzbek men and women modern ideas of citizenship and responsible political governance. It is true that the Soviet political regime did not measure up to these ideals and made every effort to distort and manipulate them to justify its one-party rule. But concepts of citizenship rights and political accountability, which are essential for a modern democratic state, are familiar to the educated urban-dwelling Uzbeks who feed the ranks of the intelligentsia. In addition, Uzbekistan benefits from numerous examples of functioning democracies and a plethora of international agencies committed to the promotion of democracy and human rights in the post-Soviet space. Other states in the former Soviet Union, as well as in Latin America and Southeast Asia, have benefited, to varying degrees, from this international commitment to the promotion of liberal democracy. The Uzbek experience is not unique. This, of course, goes against the grain of President Karimov's claim regarding the 'Uzbek path to independence'.

Such claims of authenticity rest on the elusive foundation of cultural uniqueness. The Uzbek leadership has been systematically promoting Uzbek culture as part of the drive to consolidate its nationalist credentials, even institutionalising aspects that are deemed compatible with the state system, a practice that is replicated to varying degrees in other Central Asian states. The cases of hakims and *aqsaqals* were the most vivid examples of this effort to indigenise the state. The transition from one-party rule to one-man rule, therefore, is presented as a natural process of bringing politics into line with the state's interpretation of Uzbek culture and traditions. The disguised message in this process, to put it bluntly, is that Uzbek culture is not democratic and not ready to challenge authority. Dissent is not the Uzbek way. Defying authority, whether at the local level in relation to *aqsaqals* or at the national level in relation to President Karimov, goes against the grain of Uzbek culture. This interpretation is reinforced by reference to Islam. Submission, Uzbek commentators and leaders argue, is the meaning of Islam and the mortar that keeps the Muslim Uzbek society together. This subtext offers justification for the absence of opposition parties. Not surprisingly, various government announcements about the pace of reforms have made repeated references to cultural impediments. The leadership claims to be genuine about its efforts to democratise, but constrained by the cultural framework that, allegedly, does not accommodate drastic changes in the way the state operates.[2]

An example of political culture in action may be the status of the media in Uzbekistan. Since independence, Uzbek leaders have repeatedly invited the media to act in the interests of the people, a vague notion that could be interpreted in two diametrically opposed ways – depending on whether people's interests are judged compatible with the leadership's behaviour. Following his re-election in January 2000, President Karimov delivered a notable address to the legislative assembly. It was remarkable for its carefully chosen rhetoric and for striking a chord with Western critics of Uzbekistan's political system. After emphasising the importance of liberalisation and exalting the virtues of the multiparty system, Karimov urged lawmakers not to be afraid of political opposition and to promote political pluralism and support non-governmental organisations. He then turned to the role of the media:

> The fourth question is to ensure conditions for different ideas and diverse views and for their free expression. I repeat that the media must turn into a genuine fourth estate of the realm and be the most influential factor in citizens exercising their political rights and freedoms. It is above all to ensure every citizen a chance to express their views freely, to receive information and the right to actively participate in a debate of very important issues of state and society building.[3]

Following this lead, the head of the state-run Foundation for the Democratization of the Mass Media, Abbos Alimboyev, gave an interview to the Uzbek-language newspaper *Hurriyat* in March 2000 and dismissed Uzbek newspapers as 'boring and unreadable'.[4] He criticised journalists' lack of investigative vigour and the press for its passive approach to current affairs, which contribute to the 'lack of social initiatives in Uzbekistan'. Despite appropriate legal frameworks to protect free journalism, Alimboyev argued, social liberalisation was moving very slowly. It was perhaps no coincidence that this public exposition of the Uzbek regime's commitment to democratisation and media freedom came on the eve of a visit by the US Secretary of State Madeleine Albright.

While there may have been little evidence to interpret the year 2000 announcements as anything but window dressing, new developments in 2002 seemed to suggest some tangible movement towards easing state control. In February 2002 the presidential press service invited the heads of radio and television, and chief editors of leading newspapers, to ensure that the media were more than 'observers': they should take a more proactive role in setting the agenda for public discourse.[5] This was followed by the abolition of pre-publication censorship in May 2002. This move delighted the US administration, which had argued the merits of positive engagement. The practical implications of abolishing formal censorship, however, remain limited. Self-censorship, which is encouraged by the state, as discussed in Chapter 6, has come to replace official censorship. This shift appears to confirm cultural arguments that emphasise the importance of preserving social harmony and order in Uzbek traditions and to reject actions that could be socially disruptive. The media, as an important player with a social conscience, therefore, are expected to promote the virtues of Uzbek culture, not undermine them. As a result, it has become even more important for journalists to know, instinctively, the limits of public discourse.

This aversion to what is conventionally dubbed 'socially disruptive' behaviour in Uzbekistan has been a governing principle. For over a decade, Uzbek authorities argued against a rush towards economic liberalisation and privatisation for fear of releasing untamed forces that would throw Uzbekistan into mayhem and social upheaval. President Karimov was adamant that Uzbekistan needed to avoid the Russian experience of rapid economic transformation, which resulted in the disintegration of the social security system, a sudden jump in unemployment and the creation of poverty. The Russian model of economic reform and transition to the market, President Karimov told journalists, has little regard for the social and material well-being of the people.[6] Consequently, in the Uzbek vision, reforms had to be carried out in 'a civilized manner ... without social malaise and widespread poverty, or anarchy'.[7] Gradualism, not 'shock therapy', was promoted as the 'Uzbek way'. This entailed the retention of the state as the 'main player in the economy' and the adoption of an 'evolutionary approach to reforms'. President Karimov elaborated on this theme in his book *Uzbekistan's Path to Deepening Economic Reforms*, where he identified the responsibility of the state as providing 'social security' and 'achieving economic stability in order to ensure social and political harmony in Uzbekistan'.[8]

The above concern with maintaining social security is clearly tied to the paternalistic image that the Uzbek state is keen to construct for itself. Just as the state presents itself as the guardian of Uzbek tradition, by incorporating the *mahalla* and *aqsaqals* in the administrative hierarchy of power it adopts gradualism and 'socially oriented' economic reforms to sustain the favoured image of benevolence. This is the soft side of authoritarianism, which is just as pivotal to the sustenance of the ruling regime as its iron-fist policies of repression.

Gradualism, however, is not simply a matter of symbolism. The concern with the political repercussions of a sudden rise in inflation, unemployment and poverty is very real. Aleksei Malashenko of the

Moscow Carnegie Centre has argued that macroeconomic reforms, which would inevitably take the form of 'shock therapy', have the potential to polarise society and undermine traditional bonds, with serious risks to the ability of the regime to rule. Drawing parallels with the Middle East, Malashenko has pointed to the danger of Islamic extremism and revolutionary ideas that would find a ready audience in an environment of economic despair.[9] Such a bleak environment, it may be argued, already exists in the densely populated Ferghana Valley, even though the state has steered clear of 'shock therapy'.

Over a quarter of Uzbekistan's population is concentrated in the Ferghana Valley, which covers less than 5 per cent of the republic's territory.[10] As a result, the population density in the Valley is over 340 people per square kilometre, compared with the national average of just over 53 people. Not surprisingly, despite government efforts to shield the population from the adverse effects of economic slow-down since the Soviet collapse, the impact of economic stagnation is keenly felt in the Ferghana Valley. According to a late 1990s' study, 'an estimated 35 per cent of the work force in the Uzbekistan part of the Valley is unemployed, including the majority of those under the age of twenty-five'.[11] This bleak picture may explain, to some degree, the emergence and continued activity of radical Islamic groups in the Ferghana Valley. This region was the scene of activity for a host of Islamist groups in the final days of the Soviet Union and more recently for Hizb ut-Tahrir. There is a universal consensus among observers of Central Asia that any Islamic challenge in Uzbekistan would be centred around the Ferghana Valley.

Risk assessments on the prospects of social instability and political backlash in conditions of major economic upheaval were put to the test following the October 2003 announcement by the minister of the economy and the Central Bank of Uzbekistan that the sum, the Uzbek currency, would be made fully convertible.[12] The IMF had pressed Uzbekistan for currency convertibility for years to no avail. This announcement was met with surprise as it was widely expected that Uzbekistan would continue to stonewall currency reforms, fearing price hikes and inflation. No doubt the regime hopes that the new policy of currency liberalisation will facilitate much greater foreign investment in the Uzbek economy and offset its negative repercussions. It remains to be seen if this expectation bears fruit. In the meantime, it may be asked whether currency convertibility will become the thin end of the wedge that cracks the regime's hold on the economy, and by extension society. Will this latest economic reform chip away at authoritarianism?

Responding to journalists on the implications of this decision for the price of household goods, the deputy prime minister and minster for the economy, Rustam Azimov, stated: 'we cannot guarantee stability of prices because that is not the task of the government ... we can guarantee that there will not be any intervention in the monetary and inflation process from the side of the government and Central Bank'.[13] This statement would have been unthinkable until recently, and many ordinary Uzbeks must wonder what it actually means. The notion of direct government responsibility for the welfare of the population has been a central tenet of the Soviet and post-Soviet experience and there is widespread expectation that this commitment will continue. Abandoning this responsibility would serve a blow to the paternalist image of the regime and erode its ability to claim benevolence.

It may be too early to judge the broader impact of currency convertibility. It is possible that Azimov was speaking directly to the IMF when responding to journalists. The Uzbek leadership has a demonstrated ability to adopt the jargon of liberalism when dealing with Western agencies. Azimov's guarantee on behalf of the government not to interfere with prices could have been designed to placate sceptics in Western financial centres. However, as symbolic as the above statement may have been, it is symptomatic of a shift in style on the part of the government. The regime's tight grip on the political scene has been founded on the premiss that any relaxation of state control would allow undesirable forces, generally dubbed Islamic extremism, to step up their activity. The interests of the ruling regime and those of dissidents are seen as mutually exclusive; hence any gain by the latter in the public sphere has been interpreted as a loss for the political leadership. This political philosophy has informed the attitude of the regime. Uzbek authoritarianism is founded on an understanding of exclusivity – an understanding that went beyond the political sphere and was persistently applied to the economy. It is no exaggeration, therefore, to suggest that the government's apparent withdrawal from the financial sector holds major potential implications for the foundations of authoritarianism in Uzbekistan.

It is no secret that the United States lobbied Uzbekistan for compliance with IMF recommendations. Tashkent's decision to sign Article Eight of the IMF charter, which governs currency convertibility, followed years of negotiation. The expected withdrawal of state control over prices, therefore, may be directly attributed to the US policy of patient diplomacy. This may be hailed in Washington as the first step towards reform. But it is highly unlikely that Uzbek authorities would follow the same reform agenda in the political sphere. The regime may grudgingly be giving ground to Western advocates of economic liberalisation; yet when it comes to political openness they feel threatened by freedom of speech, freedom of association and public accountability. The separation of economic and political liberalisation is not unique to Uzbekistan. The best example of such disengagement is China, and indeed Uzbek authorities have looked to the Chinese model with interest from the early days of independence. It was this salient interest in the Chinese model that led Stanislav Zhukov of the Russian Academy of Sciences to characterise Uzbekistan as a state that combines 'strict authoritarian power' with gradual economic reform.[14] It is far from certain, however, that the regime is in a position to pacify the impending backlash that is likely to surface in the wake of genuine economic reforms.

Commentators concur that the deterioration of economic conditions in Uzbekistan would create a dangerous situation. The almost inevitable drop in living standards that would follow economic liberalisation, at least in the short term, would provide a conducive environment for the spread and propagation of extremist views. In such a scenario the Uzbek regime would be increasingly restricted in its ability to preserve the soft face of its authoritarian rule and is likely to rely exclusively on the mechanisms of repression and persecution to deal with voices of discontent. Authoritarian rule without effective social security would be a weaker form of authoritarianism. If the Uzbek leadership does indeed carry out its promise, made in October 2003, and continues on that trajectory of gradual economic liberalisation, one might expect serious political repercussions for Uzbekistan and knock-on effects internationally.

The role that the United States has played in propping up the Uzbek leadership in the post-September 11 era, and its military presence in the republic and in neighbouring states, have entangled Washington in the unpredictable politics of Uzbekistan. Washington has chosen the 'lesser of two evils' and has opted to work with President Karimov's authoritarian regime against Islamism.[15] This strategy appears to have paid off for the time being as the IMU seems to have been effectively suppressed – open Islamic activism has substantially declined. In the long term, however, the consequences of this choice could be even more harmful for the prospects of political stability in Uzbekistan and US security. There have already been reports that members of Hizb ut-Tahrir are increasingly questioning the principle of nonviolence and see unabated state repression as making political violence inevitable. In addition, there is a swelling backlash against economic malaise and growing poverty. Popular discontent is likely to go beyond the Uzbek leadership and affect the United States for its role in promoting economic liberalisation. By the same token, US ties with Tashkent are widely interpreted by the ruling regime and its opponents as an endorsement of President Karimov's authoritarian rule. Washington is now seen as the international mainstay of the Uzbek regime. This association makes the United States an immediate target for the political opponents of President Karimov. The US–Uzbek partnership has helped internationalise the domestic politics of Uzbekistan.

This is not the first time that such a transformation has taken place. A very similar pattern is evident in the Middle East where unpopular rulers are supported by the United States in a transparent policy to maintain order. Islamism in the Middle East has been an underlying concern for successive US administrations, especially since the 1979 Islamic Revolution in Iran when Washington lost a regional ally to a popular revolution. The consequent alarm at the potential of Islamists to capture the state has become salient in US foreign policy towards the Muslim world.[16] This policy prioritised the preservation of the status quo in friendly countries over political transformation. The emphasis on protecting friendly rulers in power against their domestic political opponents, often manifested in Islamic forms, has seriously damaged Washington's image in the region. The United States is seen not as a force for democratisation and justice, but as a pillar for authoritarian rulers. Washington, to put it crudely, has sacrificed liberal ideals of political pluralism and freedom in the Middle East at the altar of the status quo for fear of allowing the proliferation of Islamism. As a result Washington is widely held responsible in the Middle East for the continued rule of corrupt and undemocratic regimes.

Washington's security agenda in Central Asia, since the onset of the 'war on terror', has all the hallmarks of its policy in the Middle East. Prioritising security concerns over democratisation is the defining characteristic of US policy towards the region. The similarities are ominous. Indeed Pauline Jones Luong refers to the current transformation of the political landscape as the 'Middle Easternisation of Central Asia'.[17] This should be a real concern for US policymakers. Such transformation opens up Central Asia, especially Uzbekistan, with the largest population in the region, to the international Islamist agitation that has so far been alien to these Muslim societies. Organisations such as Hizb ut-Tahrir, with their transnational networks and agenda, benefit from an environment that allows them to make a direct link between local grievances and the policies of the United States.

The security partnership between the United States and Uzbekistan against Islamism threatens to sow the seeds of discord in this Central Asian republic. It tends to confirm a dichotomous world-view, held by many Islamists, that divides the world between suppressed Muslim communities and corrupt usurpers of power who are supported by the West. Continued state suppression of dissent in Uzbekistan and the reluctance of the United States to challenge President Karimov's leadership over violations of human rights and the absence of political openness only reaffirm the above perspective. It would not be too difficult for Hizb ut-Tahrir, therefore, to argue that opposition to the present regime in Uzbekistan is part of a broader conflict between the Muslim world and the United States. This is a forceful argument and could be attractive to many Uzbeks, especially those who have suffered economic dislocation or have an alternative political agenda. The latter may not necessarily be Islamic. The history of Islamism in Uzbekistan and the rest of Central Asia has demonstrated close cooperation between Islamic and secular opposition activists. It is not difficult to imagine that many moderate, non-religious dissidents would be driven to more extremist views by the intolerant policies of the Uzbek regime. Consequently, it does not require too much imagination to foresee a deepening of the crisis of legitimacy for the Uzbek leadership and Washington if Uzbekistan continues on its present path of authoritarianism with the tacit approval of the United States.

Notes

1. Contributions of Central Asian Nations to the Campaign Against Terrorism, Hearing before the Subcommittee on Central Asia and South Caucasus of the Committee on Foreign Relations, United States Senate, One Hundred Seventh Congress, First Session, 13 December 2001 (Washington: US Government Printing Office, 2002), available at www.access.gpo. gov/congress/senate.

2. The question of compatibility between Uzbek culture and modern democracy is highly contentious. Gregory Gleason has argued that 'Uzbeks have a distinct style of behaviour, ... Uzbekistan celebrates traditions of hierarchy and authoritarianism ... it is considered gracious to obey, impolite to disagree, treacherous to oppose ... open political contestation is considered foreign.' Gregory Gleason, The Central Asian States: Discovering Independence (Boulder, CO: Westview Press, 1997), pp. 117–18. Although Gleason does not make a direct connection between the cultural traditions of submission and Uzbekistan's 'authoritarian populism', and cannot in any way be accused of being an apologist for the Karimov regime, it is precisely these traditions that the leadership invokes to justify the present state of affairs. The obvious flaw in this representation of culture, however, is that it allows little room for change and evolution.

3. President Karimov's address was broadcast on Uzbek Television first channel on 22 January 2000. See 'Uzbek President Addresses Parliament', Uzbekistan Daily Digest, www.EuasiaNet.org, 24 January 2000.

4. Abbos Alimboyev went on to talk about the value of 'oriental democracy', but did not explain what that meant. Hurriyat, 10 March 2000.

5. Narodnoye Slovo, 27 February 2002.

6. S. Novoprudskii, 'Predvaritel'nye itogi: v respublike sravnitel'no spokoino', Nezavisimaya Gazeta, 24 July 1992, p. 3.

7. Pravda, 5 August 1993, p. 1.

8. Excerpts in Ruben Safarov, 'S tochnym pritselom', Pravda Vostoka, 4 July 1995, p. 2.

9. Aleksei Malashenko, 'Islam, Politika i Bezopasnost' Tsentral'noi Azii', Svobodnaya Mysl', vol. 21, no. 3, 2003, p. 32.

10. The Ferghana Valley covers parts of three republics: Uzbekistan, Tajikistan and Kyrgyzstan.

11. Nancy Lubin et al., *Calming the Ferghana Valley* (New York: Century Foundation Press, 1999), p. 65.

12. RFE/RL, *NewsLine*, 10 October 2003.

13. RFE/RL, *Central Asia Report*, 17 October 2003.

14. Stanislav Zhukov, 'Economic Development in the States of Central Asia', in Boris Rumer, ed., *Central Asia in Transition: Dilemmas of Political and Economic Development* (Armonk: M.E. Sharpe, 1996), p. 119.

15. Boris Rumer, 'The Powers in Central Asia', *Survival*, vol. 44, no. 3, Autumn 2002, p. 66.

16. Writing on US policy towards the difficult Israeli–Palestinian conflict in the wake of the Islamic Revolution in Iran, Vaughn P. Shannon argues: 'Losing one of its major "pillars" of the region to hostile Islamic fundamentalism, the US saw new importance in propping up existing regional allies, including Israel.' Vaughn P. Shannon, *Balancing Act: US Foreign Policy and the Arab–Israeli Conflict* (Aldershot: Ashgate, 2003), p. 78.

17. Pauline Jones Luong, 'The Middle Easternization of Central Asia', *Current History*, October 2003, pp. 333–40.

Postscript

In March 2004, the sound of gunfire and explosions in Tashkent and Bukhara shook the placid tranquillity of Uzbekistan. Over thirty people were reported killed. The government blamed the incidents on the Islamic Movement of Uzbekistan, but no one has claimed responsibility. Little is known about the circumstances surrounding these events. This has led to the spread of conspiracy theories which implicate the Uzbek security forces in a plot to retain the 'Islamic threat' and encourage the long-term presence of US forces in the region. There is no evidence to substantiate this claim, or that points to the continued operation of IMU cells in Uzbekistan. The ultimate consequence of these incidents, however, is likely to be a renewed determination in Washington to stay the course and not leave Uzbekistan prematurely.

The March 2004 episode in Uzbekistan came against the background of a US review of its foreign aid policy. This annual review by the US Congress requires a report by the State Department on human rights conditions in recipient countries of US assistance. The Foreign Assistance Act, which governs US aid to Uzbekistan, provides that US aid may not be offered to states which systematically violate human rights and dignity. This places US law-makers in a difficult situation.

On 25 February 2004, the US State Department's Bureau of Democracy, Human Rights, and Labor presented the Speaker of the House of Representatives and the Senate Committee on Foreign

Relations with its *Report on Human Rights Practices in Uzbekistan* – 2003. The report opens with an unambiguous statement: 'Uzbekistan is an authoritarian state with limited civil rights', and goes on to catalogue various violations of human rights. It does not mince words in its account of the limited nature of media freedom and freedom of association. It records the arbitrary arrest of dissidents, torture and the absence of fair trials. Yet, when responding to journalists at the official release of this document, Assistant Secretary of State Lorne W. Craner chose to highlight the 'positive trends' in Central Asia.

It appears that the US desire to magnify 'positive trends' in Uzbekistan is pervasive. In the immediate aftermath of the March 2004 incidents in Uzbekistan, US Congressman David Dreier told reporters in Tashkent that he was 'very encouraged from the reports that we have been seeing in the area of human rights', without offering any examples. He went on to encourage his Uzbek hosts to continue along the path of 'greater political freedoms and economic freedoms' as a 'natural and correct step'. The same message was reiterated by Frederick Starr at the annual meeting of the American–Uzbekistan Chamber of Commerce (26 May 2004) in Washington. He pointed to Uzbekistan's 'progress [in] building up civil society and ... urged the international community to have "patience" in expecting more reforms without more donor support'.

As this book goes to press, US law-makers are debating the difficult question of US aid to a country that does not satisfy the provisions of the Foreign Assistance Act by any stretch of the imagination, but is an important player in the larger scheme of US foreign policy. Against the backdrop of concerted lobbying for Uzbekistan, however, it seems unlikely that the US Congress would ban aid to this Central Asian state in the 2005 budget. The protection of human rights standards is of course important to Washington, but security concerns have the potential to supersede it. Uzbekistan is an important player in the 'war on terror' scenario. The US administration regards Uzbekistan as a vital regional partner and critical to Central Asian regional stability, and Congress shares that view. This broader consideration for regional geopolitics and Uzbekistan's importance to Washington is likely to override particular concerns with the domestic affairs of the Central Asian state.

APPENDIX A

The Constitution of the Republic of Uzbekistan,

adopted on 8 December 1992

PREAMBLE

The people of Uzbekistan,

solemnly declaring their adherence to human rights and principles of state sovereignty, aware of their ultimate responsibility to present and future generations, relying on historical experience in the development of Uzbek statehood, affirming their commitment to the ideals of democracy and social justice, recognising the priority of generally accepted norms of international law, aspiring to a worthy life for the citizens of the Republic, setting forth the task of creating a humane and democratic rule of law, aiming to ensure civil peace and national accord, represented by their plenipotentiary deputies adopt the present Constitution of the Republic of Uzbekistan.

PART ONE
FUNDAMENTAL PRINCIPLES

Chapter 1. State Sovereignty

Article 1. Uzbekistan is a sovereign democratic republic. Both names of the state – the Republic of Uzbekistan and Uzbekistan – shall be equivalent.

Article 2. The state shall express the will of the people and serve their interests. State bodies and officials shall be accountable to the society and the citizens.

Article 3. The Republic of Uzbekistan shall determine its national-state and administrative-territorial structure, its structure of state authority and administration, and shall pursue independent home and foreign policies. The state frontier and the territory of Uzbekistan shall be inviolable and indivisible.

Article 4. The state language of the Republic of Uzbekistan shall be Uzbek. The Republic of Uzbekistan shall ensure a respectful attitude toward the languages, customs and traditions of all nationalities and ethnic groups living on its territory, and create the conditions necessary for their development.

Article 5. The Republic of Uzbekistan shall have its state symbols – the flag, the emblem, and the anthem – sanctioned by the law.

Article 6. The capital of the Republic of Uzbekistan shall be the city of Tashkent.

Chapter 2. Democracy

Article 7. The people are the sole source of state power. State power in the Republic of Uzbekistan shall be exercised in the interests of the people and solely by the bodies empowered therefore by the Constitution of the Republic of Uzbekistan and the laws passed on its basis. Any seizure of powers belonging to state authority, suspension or termination of activity of the bodies of state authority, contrary to the procedure prescribed by the Constitution, as well as the formation of any new or parallel bodies of state authority, shall be regarded as unconstitutional and punishable by law.

Article 8. All citizens of the Republic of Uzbekistan, regardless of their nationality, constitute the people of Uzbekistan.

Article 9. Major matters of public and state life shall be submitted for a nation-wide discussion and put to a direct vote of the people (a referendum). The procedure for holding referendums shall be specified by law.

Article 10. The Oliy Majlis (Supreme Assembly) and President of the Republic, elected by the people, shall have the exclusive right to act on behalf of the people. No section of society, political party, public association, movement or individual shall have the right to act on behalf of the people of Uzbekistan.

Article 11. The principle of the separation of power between the legislative, executive and judicial authorities shall underlie the system of state authority in the Republic of Uzbekistan.

Article 12. In the Republic of Uzbekistan, public life shall develop on the basis of a diversity of political institutions, ideologies and opinions. No ideology shall be granted the status of state ideology.

Article 13. Democracy in the Republic of Uzbekistan shall rest on the principles common to all mankind, according to which the ultimate value is the human being, his life, freedom, honour, dignity and other inalienable rights. Democratic rights and freedoms shall be protected by the Constitution and the laws.

Article 14. The state shall function on the principles of social justice and legality in the interests of the people and society.

Chapter 3. Supremacy of the Constitution and the Law

Article 15. The Constitution and the laws of the Republic of Uzbekistan shall have absolute supremacy in the Republic of Uzbekistan. The state, its bodies, officials, public associations and citizens shall act in accordance with the Constitution and the laws.

Article 16. None of the provisions of the present Constitution shall be interpreted in a way detrimental to the rights and interests of the Republic of Uzbekistan. None of the laws or normative legal acts shall run counter to the norms and principles established by the Constitution.

Chapter 4. Foreign Policy

Article 17. The Republic of Uzbekistan shall have full rights in international relations. Its foreign policy shall be based on the principles of sovereign equality of the states, non-use of force or threat of its use, inviolability of frontiers, peaceful settlement of disputes, non-interference in the internal affairs of other states, and other universally recognised norms of international law. The Republic may form alliances, join or withdraw from unions and other inter-state organisations proceeding from the ultimate interests of the state and the people, their well-being and security.

PART TWO
BASIC HUMAN AND CIVIL RIGHTS, FREEDOMS AND DUTIES

Chapter 5. General Provisions

Article 18. All citizens of the Republic of Uzbekistan shall have equal rights and freedoms, and shall be equal before the law, without discrimination by sex, race, nationality, language, religion, social origin, convictions, individual and social status.

Any privileges may be granted solely by the law and shall conform to the principles of social justice.

Article 19. Both citizens of the Republic of Uzbekistan and the state shall be bound by mutual rights and mutual responsibility. Citizens' rights and freedoms, established by the Constitution and the laws, shall be inalienable. No one shall have the power to deny a citizen his rights and freedoms, or to infringe on them except by the sentence of a court.

Article 20. The exercise of rights and freedoms by a citizen shall not encroach on the lawful interests, rights and freedoms of other citizens, the state or society.

Chapter 6. Citizenship

Article 21. In the Republic of Uzbekistan, uniform citizenship shall be established throughout its territory. Citizenship in the Republic of Uzbekistan shall be equal for all regardless of the grounds of its acquisition. Every citizen of the Republic of Karakalpakstan shall be a citizen of the Republic of Uzbekistan. The grounds and procedure for acquiring and forfeiting citizenship shall be defined by law.

Article 22. The Republic of Uzbekistan shall guarantee legal protection to all its citizens both on the territory of the republic and abroad.

Article 23. Foreign citizens and stateless persons, during their stay on the territory of the Republic of Uzbekistan, shall be guaranteed the rights and freedoms in accordance with the norms of international law.

They shall perform the duties established by the Constitution, laws, and international agreements signed by the Republic of Uzbekistan.

Chapter 7. Personal Rights and Freedoms

Article 24. The right to exist is the inalienable right of every human being. Attempts on anyone's life shall be regarded as the gravest crime.

Article 25. Everyone shall have the right to freedom and inviolability of the person. No one may be arrested or taken into custody except on lawful grounds.

Article 26. No one may be adjudged guilty of a crime except by the sentence of a court and in conformity with the law. Such a person shall be guaranteed the right to legal defence during open court proceedings. No one may be subject to torture, violence or any other cruel or humiliating treatment. No one may be subject to any medical or scientific experiments without his consent.

Article 27. Everyone shall be entitled to protection against encroachments on his honour, dignity, and interference in his private life, and shall be guaranteed inviolability of the home.

No one may enter a home, carry out a search or an examination, or violate the privacy of correspondence and telephone conversations, except on lawful grounds and in accordance with the procedure prescribed by law.

Article 28. Any citizen of the Republic of Uzbekistan shall have the right to freedom of movement on the territory of the Republic, as well as a free entry to and exit from it, except in the events specified by law.

Article 29. Everyone shall be guaranteed freedom of thought, speech and convictions. Everyone shall have the right to seek, obtain and disseminate any information, except that which is directed against the existing constitutional system and in some other instances specified by law.

Freedom of opinion and its expression may be restricted by law if any state or other secret is involved.

Article 30. All state bodies, public associations and officials in the Republic of Uzbekistan shall allow any citizen access to documents, resolutions and other materials, relating to their rights and interests.

Article 31. Freedom of conscience is guaranteed to all. Everyone shall have the right to profess or not to profess any religion. Any compulsory imposition of religion shall be impermissible.

Chapter 8. Political Rights

Article 32. All citizens of the Republic of Uzbekistan shall have the right to participate in the management and administration of public and state affairs, both directly and through representation. They may exercise this right by way of self-government, referendums and democratic formation of state bodies.

Article 33. All citizens shall have the right to engage in public life by holding rallies, meetings and demonstrations in accordance with the legislation of the Republic of Uzbekistan. The bodies of authority shall have the right to suspend or ban such undertakings exclusively on the grounds of security.

Article 34. All citizens of the republic of Uzbekistan shall have the right to form trade unions, political parties and any other public associations, and to participate in mass movements.

No one may infringe on the rights, freedoms and dignity of the individuals, constituting the minority opposition in political parties, public associations and mass movements, as well as in representative bodies of authority.

Article 35. Everyone shall have the right, both individually and collectively, to submit applications and proposals, and to lodge complaints with competent state bodies, institutions and public representatives.

Such applications, proposals and complaints shall be considered in accordance with the procedure and within the time limit specified by law.

Chapter 9. Economic and Social Rights

Article 36. Everyone shall have the right to own property. The privacy of bank deposits and the right to inheritance shall be guaranteed by law.

Article 37. Everyone shall have the right to work, including the right to choose their occupation. Every citizen shall be entitled to fair conditions of labour and protection against unemployment in accordance with the procedure prescribed by law.

Any forced labour shall be prohibited, except as punishment under the sentence of a court, or in some other instances specified by law.

Article 38. Citizens working on hire shall be entitled to a paid rest. The number of working hours and the duration of paid leave shall be specified by law.

Article 39. Everyone shall have the right to social security in old age, in the event of disability and loss of the bread-winner as well as in some other cases specified by law.

Pensions, allowances and other kinds of welfare may not be lower than the officially fixed minimum subsistence wage.

Article 40. Everyone shall have the right to receive skilled medical care.

Article 41. Everyone shall have the right to education. The state shall guarantee free secondary education. Schooling shall be under state supervision.

Article 42. Everyone shall be guaranteed the freedom of scientific research and engineering work, as well as the right to enjoy cultural benefits. The state shall promote the cultural, scientific and technical development of society.

Chapter 10. Guarantees of Human Rights and Freedoms

Article 43. The state shall safeguard the rights and freedoms of citizens proclaimed by the Constitution and laws.

Article 44. Everyone shall be entitled to legally defend his rights and freedoms, and shall have the right to appeal any unlawful action of state bodies, officials and public associations.

Article 45. The rights of minors, the disabled, and the elderly shall be protected by the state.

Article 46. Women and men shall have equal rights.

Chapter 11. Duties of Citizens

Article 47. All citizens shall perform the duties established by the Constitution.

Article 48. All citizens shall be obliged to observe the Constitution and laws, and to respect the rights, freedoms, honour and dignity of others.

Article 49. It is the duty of every citizen to protect the historical, spiritual and cultural heritage of the people of Uzbekistan. Cultural monuments shall have protection by the state.

Article 50. All citizens shall protect the environment.

Article 51. All citizens shall be obliged to pay taxes and local fees established by law.

Article 52. Defence of the Republic of Uzbekistan is the duty of every citizen of the Republic of Uzbekistan. Citizens will be obliged to perform military or alternative service in accordance with the procedure prescribed by law.

PART THREE
SOCIETY AND THE INDIVIDUAL

Chapter 12. The Economic Foundation of Society

Article 53. The economy of Uzbekistan, evolving towards market relations, is based on various forms of ownership. The state shall guarantee freedom of economic activity, entrepreneurship and labour with due regard for the priority of consumers' rights, as well as equality and legal protection of all forms of ownership.

Private property, along with the other types of property, shall be inviolable and protected by the state. An owner may be deprived of his property solely in the cases and in accordance with the procedure prescribed by law.

Article 54. An owner shall possess, use and dispose of his property. The use of any property must not be harmful to the ecological environment, nor shall it infringe on the rights and legally protected interests of citizens, juridical entities or the state.

Article 55. The land, its minerals, fauna and flora, as well as other natural resources shall constitute the national wealth, and shall be rationally used and protected by the state

Chapter 13. Public Associations

Article 56. Trade unions, political parties, and scientific societies, as well as women's, veterans' and youth leagues, professional associations, mass movements and other organisations registered in accordance with the procedure prescribed by law, shall have the status of public associations in the Republic of Uzbekistan.

Article 57. The formation and functioning of political parties and public associations aiming to do the following shall be prohibited: changing the existing constitutional system by force; coming out against the sovereignty, territorial integrity and security of the Republic, as well as the constitutional rights and freedoms of its citizens; advocating war and social, national, racial and religious hostility, and encroaching on the health and morality of the people, as well as of any armed associations and political parties based on national or religious principles.

All secret societies and associations shall be banned.

Article 58. The state shall safeguard the rights and lawful interests of public associations and provide them with equal legal possibilities for participating in public life.

Interference by state bodies and officials in the activity of public associations, as well as interference by public associations in the activity of state bodies and officials, is impermissible.

Article 59. Trade unions shall express and protect the socio-economic rights and interests of the working people. Membership in trade unions is optional.

Article 60. Political parties shall express the political will of various sections and groups of the population, and through their democratically elected representatives shall participate in the formation of state authority. Political parties shall submit public reports on their financial sources to the Oliy Majlis or their plenipotentiary body in a prescribed manner.

Article 61. Religious organisations and associations shall be separated from the state and equal before law. The state shall not interfere with the activity of religious associations.

Article 62. Public associations may be dissolved or banned, or subject to restricted activity solely by the sentence of a court.

Chapter 14. Family

Article 63. The family is the primary unit of society and shall have the right to state and societal protection. Marriage shall be based on the willing consent and equality of both parties.

Article 64. Parents shall be obliged to support and care for their children until the latter are of age.

The state and society shall support, care for and educate orphaned children, as well as children deprived of parental guardianship, and encourage charity in their favour.

Article 65. All children shall be equal before the law regardless of their origin and the civic status of their parents. Motherhood and childhood shall be protected by the state.

Article 66. Able-bodied children who are of age shall be obliged to care for their parents.

Chapter 15. Mass Media

Article 67. The mass media shall be free and act in accordance with the law. They shall bear responsibility for trustworthiness of information in a prescribed manner. Censorship is impermissible.

PART FOUR
ADMINISTRATIVE AND TERRITORIAL STRUCTURE
AND STATE SYSTEM

Chapter 16. Administrative and Territorial Structure of the Republic of Uzbekistan

Article 68. The Republic of Uzbekistan shall consist of regions, districts, cities, towns, settlements, kishlaks and auls (villages) in Uzbekistan and the Republic of Karakalpakstan.

Article 69. Any alteration of the boundaries of the Republic of Karakalpakstan, regions, the city of Tashkent, as well as the formation and annulment of regions, cities, towns and districts shall be sanctioned by the Oliy Majlis of the Republic of Uzbekistan.

Chapter 17. Republic of Karakalpakstan

Article 70. The sovereign Republic of Karakalpakstan is part of the Republic of Uzbekistan. The sovereignty of the Republic of Karakalpakstan shall be protected by the republic of Uzbekistan.

Article 71. The republic of Karakalpakstan shall have its own Constitution.

The Constitution of the Republic of Karakalpakstan must be in accordance with the Constitution of the Republic of Uzbekistan.

Article 72. The laws of the Republic of Uzbekistan shall be binding on the territory of the Republic of Karakalpakstan.

Article 73. The territory and boundaries of the Republic of Karakalpakstan may not be altered without the consent of Karakalpakstan. The republic of Karakalpakstan shall be independent in determining its administrative and territorial structure.

Article 74. The Republic of Karakalpakstan shall have the right to secede from the Republic of Uzbekistan on the basis of a nation-wide referendum held by the people of Karakalpakstan.

Article 75. Relations between the Republic of Uzbekistan and the Republic of Karakalpakstan, within the framework of the

Constitution of the Republic of Uzbekistan, shall be regulated by treaties and agreements concluded by the Republic of Uzbekistan and the Republic of Karakalpakstan.

Any disputes between the Republic of Uzbekistan and the Republic of Karakalpakstan shall be settled by way of reconciliation.

PART FIVE
ORGANIZATION OF STATE AUTHORITY

Chapter 18. Oliy Majlis of the Republic of Uzbekistan

Article 76. The highest state representative body is the Oliy Majlis (the Supreme Assembly) of the Republic of Uzbekistan. This body exercises legislative power.

Article 77. The Oliy Majlis of the Republic of Uzbekistan shall consist of 150 deputies, elected by territorial constituencies on a multiparty basis for a term of five years.

All citizens of the Republic of Uzbekistan who have reached the age of 25 by election day shall be eligible for election to the Oliy Majlis of the Republic of Uzbekistan. Requirements of candidates shall be determined by law.

Article 78. The exclusive powers of the Oliy Majlis of the Republic of Uzbekistan shall include:

(1) the adoption and amending of the Constitution of the Republic of Uzbekistan;

(2) enactment and amending of the laws of the Republic of Uzbekistan;

(3) determination of the guidelines of home and foreign policies of the Republic of Uzbekistan and approval of long-term projects;

(4) determination of the structure and powers of the legislative, executive and judicial branches of the Republic of Uzbekistan;

(5) admission of new states into the Republic of Uzbekistan and approval of their decisions to secede from the Republic of Uzbekistan;

(6) legislative regulation of customs, as well as of the currency and credit systems;

(7) legislative regulation of the administrative and territorial structure, and alteration of frontiers of the Republic of Uzbekistan;

(8) approval of the budget of the Republic of Uzbekistan submitted by the Cabinet of Ministers, and control over its execution; determination of taxes and other compulsory payments;

(9) scheduling elections to the Oliy Majlis of the Republic of Uzbekistan and local representative bodies, and formation of the Central Election Committee;

(10) setting the date of elections for the President of the Republic of Uzbekistan on completion of his term of office;

(11) election of the Chairman and Vice-Chairman of the Oliy Majlis of the Republic of Uzbekistan;

(12) election of the Constitutional Court of the Republic of Uzbekistan;

(13) election of the Supreme Court of the Republic of Uzbekistan;

(14) election of the Higher Arbitration Court of the Republic of Uzbekistan;

(15) appointment and dismissal of the Chairman of the State Committee for the Protection of Nature of the Republic of Uzbekistan upon the nomination of the President of the Republic of Uzbekistan;

(16) ratification of the decrees of the President of the Republic of Uzbekistan on the appointment and removal of the Prime Minister, the First Deputy Prime Ministers, the Deputy Prime Ministers and the members of the Cabinet of Ministers;

(17) ratification of the decrees of the President of the Republic of Uzbekistan on the appointment and removals of the Procurator-General of the Republic of Uzbekistan and his Deputies;

(18) appointment and removal of the Chairman of the Board of the Central Bank of the Republic of Uzbekistan upon the nomination of the President of the Republic of Uzbekistan;

(19) ratification of the decrees of the President of the Republic of Uzbekistan on the formation and abolition of ministries, state committees and other bodies of state administration;

(20) ratification of the decrees of the President of the Republic of Uzbekistan on general and partial mobilisation, and on

the declaration, prolongation and discontinuance of a state of emergency;

(21) ratification and denouncement of international treaties and agreements;

(22) institution of state awards and honorary titles;

(23) formation, annulment and renaming of districts, towns, cities and regions and alteration of their boundaries;

(24) execution of other powers defined by the present Constitution.

Article 79. A session of the Oliy Majlis shall be legally qualified if it is attended by at least ⅔ of the total number of the deputies.

Article 80. The President of the Republic of Uzbekistan, the Prime Minister, and the members of the Cabinet of Ministers, the Chairmen of the Constitutional Court, the Supreme Court and the Higher Arbitration Court, the Procurator-General of the Republic and the Chairman of the Board of the Central Bank shall have the right to attend the sessions of the Oliy Majlis.

Article 81. Upon completion of its term, the Oliy Majlis of the Republic of Uzbekistan shall retain its powers until the newly elected Oliy Majlis is convened.

The first session of the newly elected Oliy Majlis of the Republic of Uzbekistan shall be convened by the Central Electoral Committee within two months of the elections.

Article 82. The right to initiate legislation in the Oliy Majlis of the Republic of Uzbekistan is vested in the President of the Republic of Uzbekistan, the Republic of Karakalpakstan through the highest body of state authority, the deputies of the Oliy Majlis of the Republic of Uzbekistan, the Cabinet of Ministers of the Republic of Uzbekistan, the Constitutional Court, the Supreme Court, the Higher Arbitration Court and the Procurator-General of the Republic of Uzbekistan.

Article 83. The Oliy Majlis of the Republic of Uzbekistan shall pass laws, decisions and other acts. Any law shall be adopted when it is passed by a majority of the total voting power of the deputies of the Oliy Majlis.

Promulgation of the laws and other normative acts shall be a compulsory condition for their enforcement.

Article 84. The Chairman and the Vice-Chairmen of the Oliy Majlis shall be elected from among the deputies of the Oliy Majlis of the Republic of Uzbekistan by secret ballot. The Chairman and the Vice-Chairmen of the Oliy Majlis shall present annual reports to the Oliy Majlis.

One of the Vice-Chairmen of the Oliy Majlis, a deputy of the Oliy Majlis of the Republic of Uzbekistan, shall represent Karakalpakstan.

The Chairman and the Vice-Chairmen of the Oliy Majlis of the Republic of Uzbekistan shall be elected for the same term as the Oliy Majlis.

No one may be elected Chairman of the Oliy Majlis of the Republic of Uzbekistan for more than two consecutive terms.

The Chairman of the Oliy Majlis of the Republic of Uzbekistan may be recalled before completion of his term of office by the decision of the Oliy Majlis of the Republic of Uzbekistan approved by more than ⅔ of the deputies of the Oliy Majlis of the Republic of Uzbekistan by secret ballot.

Article 85. The Chairman of the Oliy Majlis of the Republic of Uzbekistan shall:

(1) exercise the general direction over a preliminary review of matters to be submitted to the Oliy Majlis;

(2) convene the sessions of the Oliy Majlis and draft their agenda together with the Chairmen of the committees and commissions;

(3) preside at the sessions of the Oliy Majlis;

(4) coordinate the work of the committees and commissions of the Oliy Majlis;

(5) organize control over the execution of the laws and the decisions passed by the Oliy Majlis;

(6) direct inter-parliamentary relations and the work of the groups connected with international parliamentary organisations;

(7) nominate candidates for the posts of the Vice-Chairmen of the Oliy Majlis and the Chairmen of the committees and commissions of the Oliy Majlis;

(8) alter the composition of the committees and commissions and submit them for confirmation to the Oliy Majlis on the proposal of the Chairmen of the committees and commissions;

(9) direct the work of the organs of the press of the Oliy Majlis;

(10) approve the rules and the editorial staff of the organs of the press of the Oliy Majlis and their expense budgets;

(11) appoint and dismiss the editors of the organs of the press of the Oliy Majlis;

(12) approve the estimated allowances of the deputies and the administrative expenses of the Oliy Majlis;

(13) sign the resolutions passed by the Oliy Majlis of the Republic of Uzbekistan.

The Chairman of the Oliy Majlis of the Republic of Uzbekistan shall issue ordinances.

Article 86. The Oliy Majlis shall elect committees and commissions to draft laws, conduct preliminary review of matters to be submitted to the Oliy Majlis, and control the execution of the laws and other decisions passed by the Oliy Majlis of the Republic of Uzbekistan.

In the event of necessity, the Oliy Majlis shall form deputies, auditing and other commissions which shall function on a permanent or temporary basis.

Article 87. The expenses of the deputies connected with their work for the Oliy Majlis shall be reimbursed in prescribed manner. The deputies working for the Oliy Majlis on a permanent basis may not hold any other paid posts, nor engage in commercial activity during their term of office.

Article 88. Deputies of the Oliy Majlis shall have the right of immunity. They may not be prosecuted, arrested or incur a court-imposed administrative penalty without the sanction of the Oliy Majlis.

Chapter 19. The President of the Republic of Uzbekistan

Article 89. The President of the Republic of Uzbekistan is head of state and executive authority in the Republic of Uzbekistan. The President of the Republic of Uzbekistan simultaneously serves as Chairman of the Cabinet of Ministers.

Article 90. Any citizen of the Republic of Uzbekistan who has reached the age of 35, is in full command of the state language and has permanently resided in Uzbekistan for at least 10 years, immediately preceding the elections, shall be eligible for the post of President of the Republic of Uzbekistan. A person may not be elected to the office of President of the Republic of Uzbekistan for more than two consecutive terms.

The President of the Republic of Uzbekistan shall be elected for a term of five years.[1] He shall be elected by citizens of the Republic of Uzbekistan on the basis of universal, equal and direct suffrage by secret ballot. The procedure for electing President shall be specified by the electoral law of the Republic of Uzbekistan.

Article 91. During his term of office, the President may not hold any other paid post, serve as a deputy of a representative body or engage in commercial activity. The President shall enjoy personal immunity and protection under law.

Article 92. The President shall be regarded as having assumed office upon taking the following oath at a session of the Oliy Majlis:'I do solemnly swear to serve faithfully the people of Uzbekistan, to comply strictly with the Constitution and the laws of the Republic, to guarantee the rights and freedoms of its citizens, and to perform conscientiously the duties of the President of the Republic of Uzbekistan.'

Article 93. The President of the Republic of Uzbekistan shall:

(1) guarantee the rights and freedoms of citizens and observance of the Constitution and the laws of the Republic of Uzbekistan;

(2) protect the sovereignty, security and territorial integrity of the Republic of Uzbekistan, and implement the decisions regarding its national-state structure;

(3) represent the Republic of Uzbekistan in domestic matters and in international relations;

(4) conduct negotiations, sign treaties and agreements on behalf of the Republic of Uzbekistan, and ensure the observance of the treaties and agreements signed by the Republic and the fulfilment of its commitments;

(5) receive letters of credence and recall from diplomats and other representatives accredited to him;

(6) appoint and recall diplomats and other representatives of the Republic of Uzbekistan to foreign states;

(7) present annual reports to the Oliy Majlis on the domestic and international situation;

(8) form the administration and lead it, ensure interaction between

the highest bodies of state authority and administration, set up and dissolve ministries, state committees and other bodies of administration of the Republic of Uzbekistan, with subsequent confirmation by the Oliy Majlis;

(9) appoint and dismiss the Prime Minister, his First Deputy, the Deputy Prime Ministers, the members of the Cabinet of Ministers of the Republic of Uzbekistan, the Procurator-General of the Republic of Uzbekistan and his Deputies, with subsequent confirmation by the Oliy Majlis;

(10) present to the Oliy Majlis of the Republic of Uzbekistan his nominees for the posts of Chairman and members of the Constitutional Court, the Supreme Court, and the Higher Economic Court, as well as the Chairman of the Board of the Central Bank of the Republic of Uzbekistan, and the Chairman of the State Committee for the Protection of Nature of the Republic of Uzbekistan;

(11) appoint and dismiss judges of regional, district, city and arbitration courts;

(12) appoint and dismiss hokims (heads of administrations) of regions and the city of Tashkent with subsequent confirmation by relevant Soviets of People's Deputies; the President shall have the right to dismiss any hokim of a district or a city, should the latter violate the Constitution or the laws, or perform an act discrediting the honour and dignity of a hokim;

(13) suspend and repeal any acts passed by the bodies of state administration or hokims;

(14) sign the laws of the Republic of Uzbekistan. The President may refer any law, with his own amendments, to the Oliy Majlis for additional consideration and vote. Should the Oliy Majlis confirm its earlier decision by a majority of ⅔ of its total voting power, the President shall sign the law;

(15) have the right to proclaim a state of emergency throughout the Republic of Uzbekistan or in a particular locality in cases of emergency (such as a real outside threat, mass disturbances, major catastrophes, natural calamities or epidemics), in the interests of people's security. The President shall submit his decision to the Oliy Majlis of the Republic of Uzbekistan for confirmation within three days. The terms and the procedure

for the imposition of the state of emergency shall be specified by law;

(16) serve as the Supreme Commander-in-Chief of the Armed Forces of the Republic and is empowered to appoint and dismiss the high command of the Armed Forces and confer top military ranks;

(17) proclaim a state of war in the event of an armed attack on the republic of Uzbekistan or when it is necessary to meet international obligations relating to mutual defence against aggression, and submit the decision to the Oliy Majlis of the Republic of Uzbekistan for confirmation;

(18) award orders, medals and certificates of honour of the Republic of Uzbekistan, and confer qualification and honorary titles of the Republic of Uzbekistan;

(19) rule on matters of citizenship of the Republic of Uzbekistan and on granting political asylum;

(20) issue acts of amnesty and grant pardon to citizens convicted by the courts of the Republic of Uzbekistan;

(21) form the national security and state control services, appoint and dismiss their heads, and exercise other powers vested in him.

The President shall not have the right to transfer his powers to a state body or official.

Article 94. The President of the Republic of Uzbekistan shall issue decrees, enactments and ordinances binding on the entire territory of the Republic on the basis of and for enforcement of the Constitution and the laws of the Republic of Uzbekistan.

Article 95. Should any insurmountable differences arise between the deputies of the Oliy Majlis, jeopardizing its normal functioning, or should it repeatedly make decisions in opposition to the Constitution, the Oliy Majlis may be dissolved by a decision of the President, sanctioned by the Constitutional Court. In the event of the dissolution of the Oliy Majlis, elections shall be held within three months. The Oliy Majlis may not be dissolved during a state of emergency.

Article 96. Should the President of the Republic of Uzbekistan fail to perform his duties due to poor health, confirmed by a certificate of a State Medical Commission formed by the Oliy

Majlis, an emergency session of the Oliy Majlis shall be held within ten days. This session shall elect an acting President of the Republic of Uzbekistan from among its deputies for a term of not more than three months. In this case the general elections of the President of the Republic of Uzbekistan shall be held within three months.

Article 97. Upon completion of his term of office, the President shall be a lifetime member of the Constitutional Court.

Chapter 20. Cabinet of Ministers

Article 98. The Cabinet of Ministers shall be formed by the President of the republic of Uzbekistan and approved by the Oliy Majlis.

The head of government of the Republic of Karakalpakstan shall be an ex officio member of the Cabinet of Ministers.

The Cabinet of Ministers shall provide guidance for the economic, social and cultural development of the Republic of Uzbekistan. It should also be responsible for the execution of the laws and other decisions of the Oliy Majlis, as well as of the decrees and other enactments issued by the President of the Republic of Uzbekistan.

The Cabinet of Ministers shall issue enactments and ordinances in accordance with the current legislation. This shall be binding on all bodies of administration, enterprises, institutions, organisations, officials and citizens throughout the Republic of Uzbekistan.

The Cabinet of Ministers shall tender its resignation to the newly elected Oliy Majlis.

The procedure for the work of the Cabinet of Ministers and its powers shall be defined by law.

Chapter 21. Fundamental Principles of Local Bodies of State Authority

Article 99. The Soviets of People's Deputies led by hokims are the representative bodies of authority in regions, districts, cities and towns, except in towns subordinate to district centres, and city districts. They shall act upon all matters within their authority, in accordance with the interests of the state and citizens.

Article 100. The local authorities shall:

ensure the observance of laws, maintain law and order, and ensure security of citizens;

direct the economic, social and cultural development within their territories;

propose and implement the local budget, determine the local taxes and fees, and propose non-budget funds;

direct the municipal economy;

protect the environment;

ensure the registration of civil status acts;

pass normative acts and exercise other powers in conformity with the Constitution and the legislation of the Republic of Uzbekistan.

Article 101. The local authorities shall enforce the laws of the Republic of Uzbekistan, the decrees of the President and the decisions of the higher bodies of state authority. They shall also direct the work of the subordinate Soviets of People's Deputies and participate in the discussion of national and local matters.

The decisions of the higher bodies on matters within their authority shall be binding on the subordinate bodies.

The term of office of the Soviets of People's Deputies and hokims is five years.

Article 102. The hokims of regions, districts, cities and towns shall serve as heads of both representative and executive authorities of their respective territories.

The hokim of the region and city of Tashkent shall be appointed and dismissed by the President with subsequent confirmation by the appropriate Soviet of People's' Deputies.

The hokims of districts, cities and towns shall be appointed and dismissed by the hokim of the appropriate region, with subsequent confirmation by the appropriate Soviet of People's Deputies.

The hokims of city districts shall be appointed and dismissed by the hokim of the city, with subsequent confirmation by the city Soviet of People's Deputies.

The hokims of towns subordinate to district centres shall be appointed and dismissed by the hokim of the district with subsequent confirmation by the district Soviet of People's Deputies.

Article 103. The hokims of regions, districts, cities and towns shall exercise their powers in accordance with the principle of one-man management, and shall bear personal responsibility for the decisions and the work of the bodies they lead.

Organisation of the work and the powers of hokims and local Soviets of People's Deputies, as well as the procedure for elections to the local Soviets of People's Deputies shall be specified by law.

Article 104. The hokim shall make decisions within his vested powers which are binding on all enterprises, institutions, organisations, associations, officials and citizens on the relevant territory.

Article 105. Residents of settlements, kishlaks and aulls (villages), as well as of residential neighbourhoods (mahallyas) in cities, towns, settlements and villages shall decide all local matters at general meetings. These local self-governing bodies shall elect a Chairman (aksakal) and his advisers for a term of 2.5 years.

The procedure for elections, organisation of the work and the powers of self-governing bodies shall be specified by law.

Chapter 22. Judicial Authority in the Republic of Uzbekistan

Article 106. The judicial authority in the Republic of Uzbekistan shall function independently from the legislative and executive branches, political parties and public organisations.

Article 107. The judicial system in the Republic of Uzbekistan shall consist of the Constitutional Court of the Republic, the Supreme Court, the Higher Economic Court of the Republic of Uzbekistan, along with the Supreme Court, and the Arbitration Court of the Republic of Karakalpakstan. These courts shall be elected for a term of five years. The judicial branch also includes regional, district, town, city, Tashkent city courts and arbitration courts appointed for a term of five years. Organisation and procedure for the operation of the courts shall be specified by law. Formation of an extraordinary court shall be inadmissible.

Article 108. The Constitutional Court of tile Republic of Uzbekistan shall hear cases relating to the constitutionality of acts passed by the legislative and executive branches.

The Constitutional Court shall be elected from political and legal scholars and shall consist of a Chairman, Vice-Chairman and judges including a representative of the Republic of Karakalpakstan.

No member of the Constitutional Court, including the Chairman, shall have the right to serve simultaneously as a deputy. The Chairman and the members of the Constitutional Court may not belong to any political parties or movements, or hold any other paid posts.

The judges of the Constitutional Court shall have the right of immunity.

The judges of the Constitutional Court shall be independent in their work and subject solely to the Constitution of the Republic of Uzbekistan.

Article 109. The Constitutional Court of the Republic of Uzbekistan shall:

(1) judge the constitutionality of the laws of the Republic of Uzbekistan and other acts passed by the Oliy Majlis of the Republic of Uzbekistan, the decrees issued by the President of the Republic of Uzbekistan, the enactments of the government and the ordinances of local authorities, as well as obligations of the Republic of Uzbekistan under inter-state treaties and other documents;

(2) conform the constitutionality of the Constitution and laws of the Republic of Karakalpakstan to the Constitution and laws of the Republic of Uzbekistan;

(3) interpret the Constitution and the laws of the Republic of Uzbekistan;

(4) hear other cases coming within its authority under the Constitution and the laws of the Republic of Uzbekistan.

The judgments of the Constitutional Court shall take effect upon publication. They shall be final and shall not be subject to appeal.

The organisation and procedure of the Constitutional Court shall be specified by law.

Article 110. The Supreme Court of the Republic of Uzbekistan shall be the highest judicial body of civil, criminal and administrative law. The rulings of the Supreme Court shall be final and binding throughout the Republic of Uzbekistan.

The Supreme Court of the Republic of Uzbekistan shall have the right to supervise the administration of justice by the Supreme Court of the Republic of Karakalpakstan, as well as by regional, city, town and district courts.

Article 111. Any economic and management disputes that may arise between entrepreneurs, enterprises, institutions and organisations based on different forms of ownership, shall be settled by the Higher Arbitration Court and other arbitration courts within their authority.

Article 112. Judges shall be independent and subject solely to the law. Any interference in the work of judges in administering the law shall be inadmissible and punishable by law.

The immunity of judges shall be guaranteed by law. The Chairmen and the members of the Supreme Court and the Higher Arbitration Court may not be deputies of the Oliy Majlis of the Republic of Uzbekistan. Judges, including district ones, may not belong to any political parties or movements, nor hold any other paid posts.

Before the completion of his term of office, a judge may be removed from his post only on grounds specified by law.

Article 113. Legal proceedings in all courts shall be open to the public. Hearings in camera shall be allowed only in cases prescribed by law.

Article 114. All court verdicts shall be binding on state bodies, public associations, enterprises, institutions, organisations, officials and citizens.

Article 115. All legal proceedings in the Republic of Uzbekistan shall be conducted in Uzbek, Karakalpak, or in the language spoken by the majority of the people in the locality. Any person participating in court proceedings who does not know the language in which they are being conducted shall have the following right to be fully acquainted with the materials in the case, to have the services of an interpreter during the proceedings, and to address the court in his native language.

Article 116. Any defendant shall have the right to defence.

The right to legal assistance shall be guaranteed at any stage of the investigation and judicial proceedings. Legal assistance to citizens, enterprises, institutions and organisations shall be given by the College of Barristers. Organisation and procedure of the College of Barristers shall be specified by law.

Chapter 23. Electoral System

Article 117. All citizens of the Republic of Uzbekistan are guaranteed the equal right to vote. Every citizen shall have only one vote. Any citizen shall be eligible for election to public office.

The President and representative bodies of authority in the Republic of Uzbekistan shall be elected on the basis of universal, equal and direct suffrage by secret ballot. All citizens of the Republic of Uzbekistan under the age of 18 shall be eligible to vote. Citizens who have been legally certified as insane, as well as persons in prison, may neither vote nor be eligible for election. Any other direct or indirect infringement on the citizens' voting rights is inadmissible.

A citizen of the Republic of Uzbekistan may not simultaneously be elected to more than two representative bodies. The electoral procedure shall be specified by law.

Chapter 24. Procurator's Office

Article 118. The Procurator-General of the Republics of Uzbekistan and the procurator subordinate to him shall supervise the strict and uniform observance of the laws on the territory of the Republic of Uzbekistan.

Article 119. The Procurator-General of the Republic of Uzbekistan shall direct the centralised system of agencies of the Procurator's office.

The Procurator of the Republic of Karakalpakstan shall be appointed by the highest representative body of the Republic of Karakalpakstan and subject to confirmation by the Procurator-General of the Republic of Uzbekistan.

The procurators of regions, districts, cities and towns shall be appointed by the Procurator-General of the Republic of Uzbekistan.

The term of office shall be five years for the Procurator-General of the Republic of Uzbekistan, the Procurator of the Republic of Karakalpakstan and procurators of regions, districts, cities and towns.

Article 120. The agencies of the Procurator's Office of the Republic of Uzbekistan shall exercise their powers independently of any state bodies, public associations and officials, and shall be subject solely to the law.

While in office procurators shall suspend their membership in political parties and any other public associations pursuing political goals.

Organisation, powers and procedure for the agencies of the Procurator's Office shall be specified by law.

Article 121. On the territory of the Republic of Uzbekistan it is prohibited to set up and run any private co-operative or other nongovernmental agencies or their branches, independently conducting any operational work, investigations, inquiries or any other functions connected with combating crime.

The law-enforcement agencies may enlist the assistance of public associations and citizens to safeguard law and order, as well as the rights and freedoms of citizens.

Chapter 25. Finance and Credit

Article 122. The Republic of Uzbekistan shall have independent financial, monetary and credit systems.

The state budget of Uzbekistan shall consist of the national budget, the budget of the Republic of Karakalpakstan and local budgets.

Article 123. The Republic of Uzbekistan shall have a single taxation system. The right to determine taxes shall belong to the Oliy Majlis of the Republic of Uzbekistan.

Article 124. The banking system of the Republic of Uzbekistan shall be directed by the Central Bank of the Republic.

Chapter 26. Defence and Security

Article 125. The Armed Forces of the Republic of Uzbekistan shall be formed to defend the state sovereignty and territorial integrity of the Republic of Uzbekistan, as well as the peaceful life and security of its citizens.

The structure and organisation of the Armed Forces shall be specified by law.

Article 126. The Republic of Uzbekistan shall maintain the Armed Forces to ensure its security at a level of reasonable sufficiency.

PART SIX
PROCEDURE FOR AMENDING THE CONSTITUTION

Article 127. The Constitution of the Republic of Uzbekistan shall be amended by laws, passed by at least ⅔ of the deputies of the Oliy Majlis of the Republic.

Article 128. The Oliy Majlis of the Republic of Uzbekistan may pass a law altering or amending the Constitution within six months of submission of the relevant proposal, with due regard for its nation-wide discussion. Should the Oliy Majlis of the Republic of Uzbekistan reject an amendment to the Constitution, a repeated proposal may not be submitted for one year.

Note

1. The presidential term was extended to seven years at the February 2002 referendum.

APPENDIX B

Extracts from the Report of the
Special Rapporteur on the Question of Torture,
Theo van Boven

Submitted in accordance with Commission resolution 2002/38 Addendum to the UN Commission on Human Rights, 59th session, 3 February 2003.

Mission to Uzbekistan

1. Following a joint request by the Special Rapporteur and the Chairman-Rapporteur of the Working Group on Arbitrary Detention in June 2000, the Government of Uzbekistan in June 2002 invited the Special Rapporteur to undertake a fact-finding mission to the country within the framework of his mandate. The mission was also discussed by the President of Uzbekistan and the Secretary-General of the United Nations on the occasion of the latter's visit to the country on 18 October. The objective of the visit, which took place from 24 November to 6 December 2002, was to enable the Special Rapporteur to collect first-hand information from a wide range of contacts in order better to assess the situation regarding torture and other forms of ill-treatment in Uzbekistan and thus be in a position to recommend to the Government a number of measures to be adopted with a view to putting an end to those practices.

The Practice of Torture: Scope and Context

General issues

34. In recent years, the Special Rapporteur had received information according to which torture is widespread and targets persons suspected of having committed ordinary crimes as well as persons accused of membership in banned political or religious organisations or of having committed crimes related to their alleged religious beliefs or activities. It was alleged that law enforcement agents seek to coerce self-incriminating confessions or testimonies against third parties, to extort bribes, or to punish, humiliate or break the will of those suspected of or convicted on political or religious grounds as well as of human rights activists. Prolonged beatings, sometimes with clubs or other implements, suffocation through the use of gas masks or plastic bags, electric shocks, sexual violence, and denial of food or water were said to be common practices. It was also alleged that the criminal justice system appeared to lack procedural safeguards against abuse by members of law enforcement agencies, as it reportedly grants procurators wide powers concerning pre-trial custody and access to lawyers/relatives and to forensic evidence. Thus, over the years, a large number of individual cases have been referred for clarification to the Uzbek authorities under the mandate of the Special Rapporteur.

35. The Minister for Foreign Affairs indicated that the Government had studied and responded to all allegations submitted under the mandate. If the replies had not reached the Special Rapporteur, it was said to be due to a 'technical problem'. The State Secretary on law enforcement agencies confirmed that all communications received from the Office of the High Commissioner for Human Rights had been studied by the relevant authorities of the country and not a single allegation had been confirmed. Despite repeated requests by the Special Rapporteur for copies of the responses, at the time of writing they had not been received.

36. The Special Rapporteur also notes with concern that from his discussion with the Acting Chairperson of the Supreme Court, it became clear that requests for interim measures issued by the

Human Rights Committee, a large number of which concern death sentences based on confessions allegedly extracted under torture, had not been brought to the attention of this organ of the judiciary, which reviews all death penalty cases. The Special Rapporteur is seriously concerned at what appears to be a lack of appropriate consideration of, and action in relation to, requests on behalf of individuals at risk of torture or even of execution, or who have been victims of acts of torture.

38. The request by the Special Rapporteur to visit the country also echoed the concerns expressed by the Committee against Torture, which included '(a) the particularly numerous, ongoing and consistent allegations of particularly brutal acts of torture and other cruel, inhuman or degrading treatment or punishment committed by law enforcement personnel; (b) the lack of adequate access for persons deprived of liberty, immediately after they are apprehended, to independent counsel, a doctor or medical examiner and family members, an important safeguard against torture; (c) the insufficient level of independence and effectiveness of the procuracy, in particular as the Procurator has the competence to exercise oversight on the appropriateness of the duration of pre-trial detention, which can be extended up to 12 months; (e) the insufficient independence of the judiciary' (CAT/C/CR/28/7, para. 6). Similarly, the Human Rights Committee had indicated that it was 'gravely concerned about consistent allegations of widespread torture, inhuman treatment and abuse of power by law enforcement officials. The Committee is also concerned about the limited number of investigations into allegations of torture' (CCPR/CO/71/U2B, para. 7).

40. According to the information received from non-governmental sources, torture is being used in virtually all cases in which articles 156, 159 and 244 CC ... are invoked, in order to extract self-incriminating confessions and to punish those who are perceived by public authorities to be involved in either religious, or political, activities contrary to State interests (so-called security crimes). These provisions, which are rather vaguely worded and whose scope of application may be subject to various interpretations, are said to have been used in numerous allegedly fabricated cases and to have led to harsh prison sentences. The four crimes that, following recent amendments, are now the only capital offences are said to lead to a death sentence only if they are combined with aggravated murder charges. Evidence gathering in such cases is said to rely exclusively on confessions extracted by illegal means. It is reported that religious leaflets as well as weapons or bullets have been planted as evidence that a person belongs to banned groups such as Hizb-ut-Tahrir, a transnational Islamic movement which calls for the peaceful establishment of the Caliphate in Central Asia. It is also reported that torture and ill-treatment continue to be used against inmates convicted on such charges, inter alia to force them to write repentance letters to the President of the Republic or to punish them further.

42. Furthermore, the Special Rapporteur has received information according to which persons belonging to sexual minorities have been subjected to various forms of torture, including of a sexual nature, and harassment, and to have been arbitrarily detained with a view to threatening or punishing them and to obtaining bribes. Temporary/casual workers who offer their services on a day-by-day basis in marketplaces are also believed to have been targeted. Casual workers, including female sex workers, have allegedly been beaten or raped if they could not pay bribes. Asylum-seekers are also believed to be at risk of being forcibly returned to countries where they may be at risk of torture (refoulement) and concern was expressed over the fact that Uzbekistan has not ratified the 1951 Convention relating to the Status of Refugees.

Lack of respect for existing legal safeguards

43. The Special Rapporteur has received information according to which lawyers have frequently been barred from taking part in the criminal investigation process or from court trials. Investigators are said to have discretionary powers in deciding if and when a suspect will have access to a lawyer. Very few cases have been reported to the Special Rapporteur in which access to a lawyer was granted within 10 days after deprivation of liberty. It is also reported that privately hired lawyers are sometimes replaced by State-appointed defence lawyers, even against the wishes of their clients. A large

number of these lawyers, who are commonly referred to as 'pocket lawyers', are said to work hand in hand with investigators. It is alleged that some have witnessed or participated in the illegal use of force during interrogation and did not intervene, or, later in court, denied allegations of torture made by defendants.

46. With respect to the trial process, the lack of statutory powers and lack of independence of judges are alleged to make any defence and any torture complaint meaningless. Independent lawyers are said to be subjected to various forms of pressure and harassment with a view to making them renounce active participation in the defence of their clients. Lawyers have reportedly been threatened by judges, including in the courtroom, and visited and assaulted by law enforcement personnel, in particular after their involvement in so-called security cases. Thus, it is widely believed by defendants and the population at large that lawyers are extremely reluctant to bring torture allegations to the attention of a magistrate during trial. Procurators are believed to be all-powerful in the criminal process and to rely almost exclusively on confessions. They control MVD and SNB investigators or carry out investigations themselves, bring charges and authorize detention, monitor respect for the CPC and the conditions of detention, and prosecute in court. During trial, their indictment is said to be the – often only – basis of the conviction. The Minister of Justice stressed that the principle of equality of arms between the prosecution and the defence was enshrined in the Constitution and the CPC. However, he acknowledged that in practice, procurators had much greater weight than defence lawyers. He was fully aware that much more needed to be done in order to overcome the deficiencies of the present practice.

Aborted visit to Jaslyk colony

49. On 1 December 2002, the Special Rapporteur visited the Jaslyk colony located in the Karakalpakstan region, in the far north-west of the country. Because of the importance and size of that colony, often cited for its hardship conditions and inhuman practices, the Special Rapporteur had clearly indicated his wish to spend there at least six hours in the facility. The matter was agreed upon with the

Deputy Minister of Internal Affairs in charge of the execution of sentences (GUIN), who accompanied the Special Rapporteur during the mission. The itinerary and schedule of his visit was modified in accordance with the recommendations of the Deputy Minister, who kindly provided the Special Rapporteur's delegation with a plane. Because of the itinerary thus chosen and the timing of the flight – the plane only flies during the daytime – the Special Rapporteur was in fact unable to spend more than two hours at Jaslyk colony. As a result, the Special Rapporteur refused to inspect the colony and concentrated on a discussion with its director, in particular on the two deaths that had occurred in August 2002, and interviews with a few inmates. The Special Rapporteur noted with concern that these confidential interviews were abruptly disrupted on several occasions by the official accompanying the Special Rapporteur's delegation. The Special Rapporteur thus regrets that he was unable to carry out the visit to Jaslyk colony in a satisfactory and comprehensive manner. Jaslyk colony, which was said by its director to hold 381 prisoners at the time of the visit, is located in the Karakalpakstan desert where temperatures can reportedly reach 60°C in summer and −30°C in winter. It is extremely remote from the main inhabited centres and there is no road between the colony and the closest urban centre, Nukus. Thus, the only public transport is the train. According to the information received, there are daily trains from Tashkent to Jaslyk colony. The journey reportedly lasts over three days and costs a sum of money that a large number of relatives cannot afford.

52. The Special Rapporteur enquired more specifically about the two recent deaths in Jaslyk colony. The bodies of Khusnuddin Alimov, aged 24, and Muzafar Avazov, aged 35, who were serving 16- and 18-year sentences respectively for their involvement in Hizb-ut-Tahrir, were returned home to Tahskent for burial on 8 August 2002. Pictures were taken of Mr. Avazov's body which was visibly covered with extensive bruises and burns, the latter possibly caused by immersion in boiling water; Mr. Alimov's body was reportedly also covered with the same types of marks and injuries. The director explained that the policy of the colony is to place religious terrorists, often said to be connected with Afghanistan or Chechnya, with common criminals. Hence, when terrorists engage in proselytism and make offensive

remarks against Uzbekistan's administrative system and political leadership, fights often break out. According to the director, this is what had happened in August 2002 in the case of Khusnuddin Alimov and Muzafar Avazov. Teapots containing boiling water were said to have been thrown during the fight, which, according to the director, explained the burns. He further indicated that, like all cases of death in custody, the case had been referred to the Office of the General Procurator which had carried out an investigation, including an autopsy, and that a decision not to open criminal proceedings had been reached. The Special Rapporteur recalled that an expert forensic examination based on the photographs of Mr. Avazov's body had been carried out by a professor of forensic medicine and science at the University of Glasgow (United Kingdom) which had concluded, inter alia, that '[t]he pattern of scalding shows a well-demarcated line on the lower chest/abdomen, which could well indicate the forceful application of hot water whilst the person is within some kind of bath or similar vessel. Such scalding does not have the splash pattern that is associated with random application as one would expect with accidental scalding.' The director answered by saying that the detainees in question had a yellow/dark complexion which burns faster. Regarding the more general question of how many persons had died in custody in Jaslyk colony in recent years, the director said he could not answer the question.

Impunity

58. Widespread allegations according to which confessions are extracted by illegal means and form the basis of evidence would also seem to be substantiated by the extremely small number of acquittals. According to non-governmental sources, the acquittal of a person is seen as evidence of negligent work on the part of the investigator, the procurator and the judge in the case, which in turn would have a negative impact on their professional career, with the possibility of the institution of disciplinary proceedings. Therefore, once a person is charged, investigators are willing to resort to illegal means to obtain a confession, without which a procurator would allegedly refuse to bring a case to court. The lack of (scientific) equipment and training and an overload of cases due to the reported 100 per

cent success rate demanded by the authorities ('solved cases' criterion for promotion) is also believed to contribute to a disproportionate reliance of investigators on confessions as evidence. Furthermore, in cases of acquittal, complaints are alleged to be lodged by the procurator against the judge ... who may be dismissed after three complaints. The legal provision allowing for the dismissal of judges against whom complaints had been lodged by three procurators was reportedly removed at the September 2001 session of Parliament. Therefore, it is believed that judges rely extensively on procurators' indictments, even if torture complaints have been raised during trial. It is said that persons charged will inevitably be convicted as it is always considered possible that law enforcement officials will resort to illegal means to obtain a confession which will then become the basis for the conviction.

APPENDIX C

The Call to Jihad
by the Islamic Movement of Uzbekistan

In the name of Allah
the Most Compassionate
the Most Merciful
A Message from the General Command
of the Islamic Movement Uzbekistan

'And fight them until there is no more fitnah and the religion is all for Allah.' *Al Anfaala:* 39

The Amir (commander) of the Harakatul Islamiyyah (Islamic Movement) of Uzbekistan, Muhammad Tahir Farooq, has announced the start of the Jihad against the tyrannical government of Uzbekistan and the puppet Islam Karimov and his henchmen. The leadership of the Islamic Movement confirm the following points in the declaration:

This declaration comes after agreement by the major ulema and the leadership of the Islamic Movement.

This agreement comes based on clear evidence on the obligation of Jihad against the tawagheet as well as to liberate the land and the people.

The primary objective for this declaration of Jihad is the establishment of an Islamic state with the application of the Sharia, founded upon the Koran and the Noble Prophetic sunnah.

Also from amongst the goals of the declaration of Jihad is:

The defense of our religion of Islam in our land against those who oppose Islam.

The defense of the Muslims in our land from those who humiliate them and spill their blood.

The defense of the scholars and Muslim youth who are being assassinated, imprisoned and tortured in extreme manners-with no rights given them at all.

And the Almighty says:

'And they had no fault except that they believed in Allah, the Almighty, Worthy of all praise!' *Al Buruj: 8.*

Also to secure the release of the weak and oppressed who number some 5,000 in prison, held by the transgressors. The Almighty says:

'And what is the matter with you that you do not fight in the way of Allah and the weak and oppressed amongst men, women and children.' *An Nisaa:75.*

And to reopen the thousands of mosques and Islamic schools that have been closed by the evil government.

The Mujahedeen of the Islamic Movement, after their experience in warfare, have completed their training and are ready to establish the blessed Jihad.

The Islamic Movement warns the Uzbek government in Tashkent from propping up or supporting the fight against the Muslims.

The Islamic Movement warns tourists coming to this land that they should keep away, lest they be struck down by the Mujahedeen.

The reason for the start of the Jihad in Kyrgyzstan is due to the stance of the ruler Askar Akayev Bishkek, in arresting thousands of Muslim Uzbeks who had migrated as refugees to Kyrgyzstan and were handed over to Karimov's henchmen (i.e. Uzbek regime).

The Most High says:

'Verily the oppressors are friends and protectors to one another.'

The Islamic Movement shall, by the will of Allah, make Jihad in the cause of Allah to reach all its aims and objectives.

It is with regret that Foreign Mujahedeen (Al Ansaar) as of yet have not entered our ranks.

The Islamic Movement invites the ruling government and Karimov leadership in Tashkent to remove itself from office – unconditionally, before the country enters into a state of war and destruction of the land and the people. The responsibility for this will lie totally on the shoulders of the government, for which it shall be punished.

Allah is Great and the Honor is for Islam.

Head of the Religious Leadership of the Islamic Movement of Uzbekistan
Az Zubayr Ibn 'Abdur Raheem
4th Jumadi Al Awwal (ah)
25 August 1999

Source: Rashid Ahmed, Jihad: The Rise of Militant Islam in Central Asia (New Haven: Yale University Press, 2002), pp. 247–9.

Select Bibliography

Abdullaev, Kamoludin, and Akbarzadeh, Shahram. *Historical Dictionary of Tajikistan* (Lanham, MD: Scarecrow Press, 2002).

Akbarzadeh, Shahram. 'Islamic Clerical Establishment in Central Asia', *South Asia*, vol. 20, no. 2, December 1997, pp. 73–102.

Akbarzadeh, Shahram. 'Uzbekistan Looks West', *Russian and Euro-Asian Bulletin*, vol. 8, no. 4, April 1999, pp. 1–8.

Bennigsen, Alexandre, and Wimbush, Enders S. *Mystics and Commissars* (Berkeley, CA: University of California Press, 1985).

Blank, Stephen. 'The United States and Central Asia', in Roy Allison and Lena Jonson, eds, *Central Asian Security: The New International Context* (Washington DC: Brookings Institution Press, 2001).

Bohr, Annette. *Uzbekistan: Politics and Foreign Policy* (London: Royal Institute of International Affairs, 1998).

Brzezinski, Zbigniew. 'A Geostrategy for Eurasia', *Foreign Affairs*, vol. 76, no. 5, September–October 1997, pp. 50–65.

Brzezinski, Zbigniew. 'The premature partnership', *Foreign Affairs*, vol. 73, no. 2, March–April 1994, pp. 67–83.

Carlisle, Donald S. 'Geopolitics and Ethnic Problems of Uzbekistan and Its Neighbours', in Yaacov Ro'i, ed., *Muslim Eurasia: Conflicting Legacies* (Newbury Park: Frank Cass, 1995).

Carlisle, Donald. 'The Uzbek Power Elite: Politburo and the Secretariat, 1938–83)', *Central Asia Survey*, vol. 5, no. 3–4, 1986, pp. 91–132.

Cherniavskii, Stanislav. 'Otstaivaia Natsional'nie Interesi: Politika Rossii v Tsentral'noi Asii i Zakavkaz'e', *Svobodnaya Mysl'* 7, 2002, pp. 13–28.

Colton, Timothy J. 'Superpresidentialism and Russia's Backwater State', *Post-Soviet Affairs*, vol. 11, no. 2, 1995, pp. 144–8.

Critchlow, James. *Nationalism in Uzbekistan, A Soviet Republic's Road to Sovereignty* (Boulder, CO: Westview Press, 1991).

Dannreuther, Roland. 'Can Russia Sustain Its Dominance in Central Asia?',

Security Dialogue, vol. 32, no. 2, June 2001, pp. 245–8.

Eickelman, Dale F., and Piscatori, James. *Muslim Politics* (Princeton, NJ: Princeton University Press, 1996).

Fairbanks, Charles, Starr, S. Frederick, Nelson, C. Richard, and Weisbrode, Kenneth. *Strategic Assessment of Central Asia* (Washington, DC: The Atlantic Council of the United States, and Central Asia–Caucasus Institute, SAIS, Johns Hopkins University Press, 2001).

Fierman, William. 'Policy Toward Islam in Uzbekistan in the Gorbachev Era', *Nationalities Papers*, vol. 22, no. 1, 1994, pp. 225–46.

Fierman, William. 'Political Development in Uzbekistan: Democratization?', in Karen Dawisha and Bruce Parrott, eds, *Conflict, Cleavage and Change in Central Asia and the Caucasus* (Cambridge: Cambridge University Press, 1997).

Fish, M. Steven. 'The Executive Deception: Superpresidentialism and the Degradation of Russian Politics', in Valerie Sperling, ed., *Building the Russian State: Institutional Crisis and the Quest for Democratic Governance* (Boulder, CO: Westview Press, 2000).

Gleason, Gregory. *The Central Asian States: Discovering Independence* (Boulder, CO: Westview Press, 1997).

Gleason, Gregory. 'Inter-State Cooperation in Central Asia from the CIS to the Shanghai Forum', *Europe–Asia Studies*, vol. 53, no. 7, 2001, pp. 1077–95.

Hale, Henry. 'Islam, State-building and Uzbekistan Foreign Policy', in Ali Banuazizi and Myron Weiner, eds, *The New Geopolitics of Central Asia and its Borderlands* (Bloomington and Indianapolis: Indiana University Press, 1994).

Horsman, Stuart. 'Uzbekistan's Involvement in the Tajik Civil War 1992–97: Domestic Considerations', *Central Asian Survey*, vol. 18, no. 1, 1999, pp. 37–48.

International Crisis Group (ICG). *The IMU and the Hizb-ut Tahrir: Implications of the Afghanistan Campaign*, Central Asia Briefing, Osh/Brussels, 30 January 2002.

Ishiyama, John T., and Kennedy, Ryan. 'Superpresidentialism and Political Party Development in Russia, Ukraine, Armenia and Kyrgyzstan', *Europe–Asia Studies*, vol. 53, no. 8, 2001, pp. 1177–91.

Landau, Jacob M., and Kellner-Heinkele, Barbara. *Politics of Language in the ex-Soviet Muslim States* (London: C. Hurst, 2001).

Lapidus, Gail W. 'Central Asia in Russian and American Foreign Policy after September 11, 2001', unpublished paper presented at the University of California, Berkeley, 29 October 2001, pp. 1–7.

Lentini, Pete. 'The Shanghai Cooperation Organization and Central Asia', in Marika Vicziany, Pete Lentini and David Wright-Neville, eds, *Regional Security in the Asia Pacific: 9/11 and After* (Cheltenham: Edward Elgar, 2004).

Lubin, Nancy et al. *Calming the Ferghana Valley* (New York: Century Foundation Press, 1999).

Luong, Pauline Jones, and Weinthal, Erika. 'New Friends, New Fears in Central Asia', *Foreign Affairs*, vol. 81, no. 2, March–April 2002, pp. 61–70.

Luong, Pauline Jones. 'The Middle Easternization of Central Asia', *Current History*, October 2003, pp. 333–40.

Luong, Pauline Jones. *Institutional Change and Political Continuity in Post-Soviet Central Asia* (Cambridge: Cambridge University Press, 2002).

Malashenko, Aleksei, 'Islam, Politika i Bezopasnost' Tsentral'noi Azii', *Svobodnaya Mysl'*, vol. 21, no. 3, 2003, pp. 26–35.

Melvin, Neil J. *Uzbekistan: Transition to Authoritarianism on the Silk Road* (Amsterdam: Harwood, 2000).

Migranian, Andranik. 'Konets Rossii?', *Svobodnaya Mysl'* 7, 2002, pp. 4–12.

Oliker, Olga, and Szayna, Thomas S., eds. *Faultlines of Conflict in Central Asia and the South Caucasus* (Santa Monica, CA: Rand, 2003).

Olcott, Martha Brill. *Central Asia's New States: Independence, Foreign Policy, and Regional Security* (Washington DC: United States Institute of Peace Press, 1996).

Prokurin, Sergei. 'Mezhdunarodnye otnosheniya v postvestfal'skuyu epokhu', *Svobodnaya Mysl'* 5, 2003, pp. 64–71.

Rashid, Ahmed. *Jihad: The Rise of Militant Islam in Central Asia* (New Haven, CT: Yale University Press, 2002).

Ro'i, Yaacov. 'The Secularization of Islam and the USSR's Muslim Areas', in Yaacov Ro'i, ed., *Muslim Eurasia: Conflicting Legacies* (Newbury Park: Frank Cass, 1995).

Ro'i, Yaacov. *Islam in the CIS: A Threat to Stability* (London: Royal Institute of International Affairs, 2001).

Roy, Olivier. *The Foreign Policy of Central Asian Islamic Renaissance Party* (New York: Council on Foreign Relations, 2000).

Roy, Olivier. *The New Central Asia. The Creation of Nations* (London: I.B. Tauris, 2000).

Ruffin, M. Holt, and Waugh, Daniel (eds). *Civil Society in Central Asia* (Seattle and London: Center for Civil Society International in association with University of Washington Press, 1999).

Rumer, Boris. 'The Powers in Central Asia', *Survival*, vol. 44, no. 3, Autumn 2002, pp. 57–68.

Rywkin, Michael. 'Central Asia in the Forefront of Attention', *American Foreign Policy Interests* 24, 2002, pp. 35–42.

Shannon, Vaughn P. *Balancing Act: US Foreign Policy and the Arab–Israeli Conflict* (Aldershot: Ashgate, 2003).

Sokolov, Alexander. 'Russian Peace-keeping Forces in the Post-Soviet Area', in Mary Kaldor and Basker Vashee, eds, *Restructuring the Global Military Sector*, Vol. I (London and Washington DC: New Wars Printer, 1997).

Starr, S. Fredrick. 'Making Eurasia Stable', *Foreign Affairs*, vol. 74, no. 1, January–February 1996, pp. 80–92.

Wolfowitz, Paul D. 'Clinton's First Year', *Foreign Affairs*, vol. 73, no. 1, January–February, pp. 28–43.

Zhukov, Stanislav, 'Economic Development in the States of Central Asia', in Boris Rumer, ed., *Central Asia in Transition: Dilemmas of Political and Economic Development* (Armonk: M.E. Sharpe, 1996).

Index